Designing Clas... ...acy

Spaces
&Places

Stenhouse Publishers
Portland, Maine

Debbie
Diller

Stenhouse Publishers
www.stenhouse.com

Library of Congress Cataloging-in-Publication Data
Diller, Debbie, 1954–
    Spaces & places : designing classrooms for literacy / Debbie Diller.
    p. cm.
    Includes bibliographical references and index.
    ISBN 978-1-57110-722-0 (alk. paper)
    1. Language arts (Elementary) 2. Classroom environment I. Title.
II. Title: Spaces and places.
LB1576.D4648 2008
372.6—dc22   2008011774

Cover design, interior design, and typesetting by Martha Drury

Manufactured in the United States of America on acid-free paper
14 13 12 11 10 09 08   9 8 7 6 5 4 3 2 1

To Nancy, for her wisdom,
strength, and encouragement

Contents

v

Acknowledgments

First thanks go to the teachers from Hearne Elementary in Alief ISD in Houston, Texas, where I began this work in 1995. It was there, as we studied literacy work stations and how to help children work on their own, that I began noticing how space affects student behavior and independence. You opened your doors to me and allowed me to try new things and take photos to document the work we were doing together. Thank you from the bottom of my heart!

My deep gratitude goes out to the hundreds of teachers who have let me come into their rooms, watch their classes at work, and teach alongside them. This collaborative work has yielded the book you now hold. I can't name every teacher whose classroom is pictured in this book, although I can probably name the school where the picture was taken.

Several schools in particular asked me to work with them on classroom space, and I am indebted to all of them. In Texas, much appreciation goes to Kelly Andrews and her teachers at Don Jeter Elementary in Alvin; to Carol Suell and her teachers at Deerwood Elementary in Humble; to Raymond Stubblefield and the staff in Aldine ISD; to David Walker and Janice Powell and their teachers in Channelview ISD; and to Noel Gray and her support of classroom makeovers in Pearland ISD. In West Virginia, thanks to all of you at Nutter Fort Primary in Nutter Fort; to Jeff Pancione and the staff at Augusta Elementary in Augusta; and to Roy Wager and the folks in the Upshur County Schools. In Indiana, thanks to Karen Foster and all the educators I worked with in Warren Township in Indianapolis, for your openness to change and to spreading the word; and to my friends in

Kokomo, who listened to my ideas and put them into practice. And finally, thanks to the educators in the Norfolk Public Schools in Virginia who worked with me on classroom makeovers.

In the Houston Independent School District, I'd like to thank several principals and teachers with whom I did ongoing classroom space work, including Sue Bargaleski at Scarborough Elementary; Linda McKenzie at Durham Elementary; Jim Goggin and Janie Evans at Herod Elementary; Elena Martinez-Buley at Rodriguez Elementary; and Mechiel Rozas at Mistral Early Childhood Center. Also, deep appreciation goes to Frank Vecchio at 10th and Penn Elementary in Reading, Pennsylvania. The school is housed in a former bank building—quite a space challenge. Thank you to Tawn Ketterman and her teachers for opening their lovely rooms at Valley View Elementary in York, Pennsylvania, and to Elisa Farris and her teachers at Alexander Elementary in Katy, Texas, for all the photo ops.

Over the past few years, several individual teachers in the Houston area allowed me to visit their classrooms week after week and document processes related to organizing space for instruction. Thank you for sharing your rooms, your students, and your ideas with me. You have made this book a better one: Donna Cronan, Vicky Georgas, Lisa Gregory, Pam House, Sara Salas, Patty Terry, Heather Thrash, and Dawn Vela. Your teaching and your rooms have inspired me. Most of you had small-space challenges and worked creatively and diligently to make more space for children.

Julie Morgenstern's *Organizing from the Inside Out* (Henry Holt, 1998) changed the way I think about organizing any space, including a classroom. This book helped me better organize my office and my house, and, over time, the classrooms where I was working. Thanks, Julie, (though we've never met) for your brilliant work.

It has been my honor to work with the wonderful people at Stenhouse Publishers once again. You work magic with the ideas on these pages. A special thanks to Philippa Stratton, who thought outside the box with me to produce a book filled with colored photos, a spiral binding, and tabs—all the things teachers have been asking for. I've learned so much about being a writer from you; you make it easy by asking just the right questions, suggesting things I haven't thought of, and stepping back to let the book flow. I am blessed to work with you.

Also, a big thanks to all the Stenhouse reps, who work so hard to get these books and ideas in the hands of educators across the country. We will all miss Nancy Considine, our dear friend who recently passed. I am indebted to her for all her support and encouragement over the years and for introducing me to Stenhouse.

Finally, I'm grateful to my friends in Houston, where I live when I'm not traveling to schools across the country. A special thanks to

Tangye Stephney, my mentor and best friend, who helped me get organized and who keeps me real; to Gretchen Childs and Pam Pierce, who consult with me, work on classroom makeovers, and work with teachers in such a powerful way (even when it means getting stuck in an airport for hours on end); and to Sanita Alrey-DeBose, who helps me keep it all together.

Last but not least, to the most important people in my life: Tom, Jon, and Jess; Mom and Dad; San and Doug. You are my family, and I'm ever grateful for the time we get to spend together. Thanks for standing behind all I do.

Why Look at Classroom Space?

You walk through the door and are transported to a place where children and literacy can blossom. The space isn't big, but every inch is being utilized thoughtfully. There is a classroom library in the corner with labeled baskets of books and some cool chairs that make you want to curl up and read. On the walls are charts made by the students and teacher that show what they've been learning. There's an area for whole-group teaching and a separate space with a table for small-group teaching. This room is a place where the teacher works to meet the needs of *all* students in a variety of instructional settings, including whole group, small group, one-on-one, partner work at stations, and cooperative groups. It's a place where children are valued.

Most of us dream of this kind of classroom, where we walk in and find all the materials we need for our whole-group teaching right where they belong (instead of having to dig through a stack behind our desks), where everything we need for guided reading is organized and ready to roll in the small-group space. Our desks aren't dumping grounds, but instead are work spaces, with room to write our plans or organize our anecdotal notes. We can spend our time with children rather than losing valuable minutes looking for stuff.

Teachers often struggle with space. Our classrooms may be small or antiquated; we have lots of materials and supplies, and there's never enough room for (or time to organize) everything. Add twenty-plus children to the mix, and it can feel downright challenging!

In my work as a teacher, literacy coach, and consultant, I have seen the impact of space on instruction. No matter how long we've taught, some days are tough. Our frequent response is to rearrange our rooms after school. Maybe it just feels good to move around all that furniture and start with a whole new plan. Or perhaps we can blow off some steam as we're shifting those desks and tables to different parts of the room. Many times, changing student seating temporarily improves behavior.

One day while working as a literacy coach, it occurred to me that if we would *begin* the year with a thoughtful plan for classroom design, we wouldn't have to keep rearranging the furniture all year long. If we had a foundation of spaces that were well thought out and organized, then when we had a rough day, we could look first at classroom instruction, not classroom space. We could examine our teaching rather than our surroundings and tackle the problem that way.

Jason, a first-grade teacher, invited me into his room one day to observe his students during small-group reading instruction and literacy work stations time. He'd had trouble with students' being off-task and disturbing him during reading group, which affected his instruction. He hoped I could give some input as an outside person. As I watched his children, I noted the link between the spaces in his room and his kids' behavior. If the space was crowded or messy, kids seemed to not get along as well. When we cleaned up the area and put materials at the children's fingertips, behavior usually improved and students became more independent, since they could easily find what they needed.

For example, the writing table contained broken pencils and paper strewn all over the place, and it was difficult for kids to find what they needed. We took a few minutes as a class to organize this space. Jason provided stacking trays for paper and cups for writing utensils, and the children helped make labels for the containers. They worked with Jason to write an "I Can" list, jotting down what they *could* do at that station. The teacher provided the structure and then gave kids the opportunity to share the ownership for that space. Student behavior and time-on-task improved greatly.

In an upper-grade classroom, Amy had difficulty having small-group instruction because her small-group table was stacked with papers and projects. When I asked about redoing her space, her eyes lit up. "You know how much I want to teach well in small group?" she said. "But I can't get to it with all this stuff that keeps piling up." It was her job to provide the structure for small group, but she couldn't easily get to what she needed to successfully teach her lessons.

One afternoon we stayed after school and systematically went through everything on her table. We threw away old junk, filed things that needed to be put away, and stored materials with no home in containers. Once this area was cleaned up, Amy had a spot in which she could easily teach, and her small-group instruction took place regularly. She had places for all her materials; kids could easily grab the pencils, dry erase materials, and books required for their lessons. At the end of each small-group meeting, students helped Amy return things where they belonged. It had become *their* space to learn with each other.

In the fall I visited Maria, a primary teacher who admitted that she really didn't like the way her room felt. "Every day when I come in here, my desk screams for me to clean it up. But there's just no time. I can barely keep up with all the paperwork I must do. I don't really like how my room looks or the way I'm teaching. If you can help me, I'd like to keep teaching. If not, I might look for a new career." Using a classroom mapping tool I designed, we took a look at her room, one area at a time, and redid her space. When the students entered the room the next day, they were excited about the new arrangement. Maria had structured the space. Now it was time for the kids to help make the space theirs. They worked together to sort the books in the classroom library. As a class, they created anchor charts for the walls. They suggested books and tools they wanted to practice with in the Big Book station. They told their teacher what materials they thought would help them in each area. The change was amazing. Maria's teaching transformed; she began using literacy work stations and small group since she now had space for them; when her teammates saw what she was trying, they followed suit. And the kids took ownership for their learning.

In this book, you'll find before and after pictures that show how we changed spaces like this, plus step-by-step instructions on how to do it. Restructuring classroom spaces often leads to improved instruction. It provides the structure necessary for instruction to be more successful and allows kids to add their stamp and make the room theirs.

Where Did the Ideas in This Book Come From?

Time and time again, teachers have asked me for help in organizing their classrooms. As I taught them how to teach in whole-group, small-group, and literacy work stations, it became clear that setting up space had to be a priority. Teaching in a well-organized area facilitated more effective (and efficient) instruction.

As I explored the topic of space, I collected questions on sticky notes from educators in hundreds of classrooms I visited and workshops I presented. (See Figure I.1.) Using these as a springboard, I worked with teachers to develop step-by-step processes for setting up the classroom spaces found on the pages of this book. These ideas worked in all kinds of places—large and small classrooms, urban and suburban schools, open and closed areas, old schools and new, kindergarten and fifth grade, portable buildings, and even a converted bank building. Here are some questions and comments that inspired me:

> "What do I *really* need in my room? I keep everything!"
>
> "What can I get rid of?"
>
> "How can I set up literacy work stations? I don't think I have enough space."
>
> "Could you help my teachers use their space better? And possibly help me with my desk?"
>
> "I could teach like that if I had *all* that room!"
>
> "Those rooms in your videos are *so* big. No wonder they look so good."
>
> "Where did you hide all the teacher's stuff?"
>
> "You mean that six filing cabinets is too many in my room?"
>
> "But . . . I might need it some day!"

You will find solutions to all these questions and comments on the following pages. You'll also read about things I never dreamed I'd study—how to pack up at the end of the year, how to prepare for a move, and how to reenvision your storage areas. Some processes involve having the kids help you; others you'll have to do on your own. Wherever possible, we involved students in the process of helping us with space. I found that with elementary students, it is our responsibility to lay the foundation and the structure first, then we can invite the kids to help us.

A teacher I coached had taught for over twenty years in the same grade in the same classroom. She had amassed quite a collection of stuff. I went through the items with her in each area of the room and helped her see that she could get rid of some of them. Eventually, she was enjoying her clutter-free space. Her newly organized surroundings helped pave the way for her to try some new instructional ideas, like small-group instruction and literacy work stations. It took time, but she appreciated the ownership her students took for their learning as she slowly released more control to them. She set up the space and then invited students to help.

This book is quite different from previous books I've written because the information is provided in photos rather than text. This was intentional. Teachers told me they liked the photos from my other books but wanted larger, colored pictures that would show more details. In addition, research has taught us that the brain thinks in pictures. We teach students to visualize to help them comprehend. Because this book is about space (and how it impacts instruction), it needed to be visual. It is my hope that you will read the pictures *and* the words (just like we ask our kids to do). It will increase your comprehension of how space impacts instruction.

So How Does Classroom Environment Affect Instruction?

When working in schools across the country, I take notes about my observations so that I can use them to reflect on afterward. I keep a writer's notebook each time I study a new topic (such as space). Here are some excerpts from my notes on classroom space:

Aug. 31—*Today I noticed how classroom environment influenced my instruction. In kindergarten, I planned my modeled lesson around using children's names in our writing, since the teacher had kids' names posted all around the room in accessible places. Using their names helped students take ownership of the learning. They loved using their names. We wrote together on a large chart at their eye level. When we were done, they could look back at the chart for help as they wrote on their own. As we shared at the end of writing time, one student asked if we could put the chart in the names station to help them with their writing. Kids always have the best ideas . . . if we invite them to be part of the learning.*

Feb. 4—*I helped some teachers work with their classroom space today. Some rooms were very cluttered. Teachers said that when they moved in, they kept everything because they didn't know they could get rid of stuff. After sharing ideas for how to organize their space, they said they'd start to clean out closets and then move things they found into their classrooms for teaching. By doing this, they'd have more space for students. They were excited for a new start. They were ready to put some of my ideas for sharing the learning with kids once the room was structured for this to happen.*

I also did a classroom makeover in David's room. Here are the questions I asked him:
- *What literacy work stations do you want to have? Why?*
- *Where will you put these? Why?*
- *How will these link to instruction?*
- *How will you structure them for independence?*
- *How will you share the ownership with students?*

I've found that what we have easy access to we use more readily. When materials are at our fingertips, it's easier to teach and we get more out of our instruction. We can teach more fluently and accomplish more if we don't have to run across the room to find something. We can use those precious extra minutes of teaching to involve our students in the learning (rather than doing everything for them to save time).

Worksheets also affect time, space, and learning in the classroom. Teachers who use lots of worksheets often have stacks of paper all around their rooms, which take up valuable space and can keep kids from thinking independently. By relying on worksheets for all student practice, we remove opportunities for students to be responsible for their learning. It's all about us—choosing the papers, running them off, keeping up with them, and grading them. Instead, I use literacy work stations as part of independent practice—so kids can use spaces around the classroom to get up, think with a partner, and practice together.

Likewise, word walls that are out of reach in high places are rarely effective for teaching. Students can't access them, and it's hard for teachers to change words because they're hard to reach. By placing your word wall where you and your students can reach it, it can become a teaching tool for everyone to use. My friend Lisa has her third-grade kids create word wall cards. The class chooses interesting words, and individual students write each word on a card and illustrate it before adding it to the wall. This is a word wall the students own and use.

Across upper grade levels, the whole-group teaching area often starts to disappear. But I've found that it is possible to keep this space available for older kids during modeled lessons. In fact, students usually seem to pay better attention here than at their desks. During one staff development session, an upper-grade special education teacher commented, "I love the idea of kids sitting together on the floor for part of instruction. It makes them feel like a part of the group, and special ed kids seldom feel like they are a part of anything." Yet another reason for planning classroom space: to make kids feel like they're part of the learning.

In addition, principals I've worked with have told me that changing the environment of the classroom definitely helps reduce discipline problems. Too much stuff on the walls can exacerbate distraction, especially for kids affected by attention deficit disorder. Many times that stuff on the walls comes from a teacher supply store (rather than from the students). A whole-group teaching area can bring kids closer for instruction and keep them from playing at their desks. Thoughtful attention to designing a classroom for instruction can head off many problems at the pass. Moving a taller piece of furniture from the middle of the classroom can create a more open space and allow the teacher to observe the whole class while she works with a small group.

Many teachers have too much furniture in their rooms, which takes up valuable "kid space." Do you have some old shelves from home that are falling apart? Or perhaps a ragged chair? Maybe you have some extra tables, "just in case." Seasoned teachers have admitted to me they hoard furniture because they fear if they get rid of it, they'll never get it again. The problem is, it's taking up room that could be used by children.

Removing extra and unsightly furniture can open up the classroom for change. In fact, this book is all about change: change in space to create structure for teaching that can open up opportunities to involve your children in the learning. My hope is that the photos, accompanying charts, and questions for reflection at the end of each chapter will inspire you to try some new things in your classroom.

Do I Have to Be Naturally Organized to Teach Like This?

Absolutely not. In fact, I am a stacker and a collector, by nature. I have to fight hard to get and stay organized. Being organized has become a priority for my life because it allows me to accomplish so much more. When my space is organized, it gives me a sense of calm and control.

In 2000, I quit my teaching job and started my own consulting business. My best friend, Tangye, told me she'd come over and help me get organized. She knew how much stuff I owned and that I am a "recovering clutterholic." She sat beside me and helped me throw away materials I'd clung to from as far back as 1976, the year I began teaching, including the ABC train I'd painstakingly drawn, laminated, and cut out during my early years. Did it hurt to throw it away? No. In fact, it felt good.

My friend (and my cleanup) gave me permission to move on with my teaching life. Once I got started, I was on a roll. It was actually cathartic to get rid of things I'd not used in years. It made room for my new career and an exciting fresh start. Tangye helped me set up a system for storing my materials. It was amazing to see how much space we found when we kept only what was most important. Since then I've learned to take a thoughtful look at the purposes for every space in our rooms, including the walls, the tables, the desks, the floor, and so forth. Over time, I learned how to become more organized. So can you, even if you're not naturally inclined this way. And as an added bonus, we are modeling for students how to create organized spaces, which will help them as learners over the years, too.

How Can Rethinking My Space Help My Teaching?

By thinking about how space is used in our classrooms, we have to think about instructional priorities. Sometimes we've wanted to try a new teaching technique, such as using a word wall, but it's not until we take time to figure out how it will work in our classroom space that we feel organized enough to take on that added challenge. Several summers ago, I suggested to Mrs. Fields, a principal whose school I consulted with, that we might set up two classrooms to give teachers an idea of how to better utilize their space for small-group teaching. She was reluctant at first, but agreed and selected two teachers whose rooms needed weeding or better organization. She also moved those teachers to brand-new rooms for the following year, so they could think about their space in new ways.

We invited all the teachers at those grade levels to come and be part of the "classroom makeover" experience. We could have called it "Fresh Start," because that's exactly what it was. We spent a half-day in each classroom, and by the end of the day the rooms had the beginning of a new look. First, we created a map of the new space. Then, as a team, we moved furniture and set up the space together. In both cases, the teachers chose to weed out old things they no longer saw a need for in their new space. They got rid of old files, faded bulletin board materials, out-of-date adoption kits, and purple ditto masters (to name a few things). We created areas for whole-group as well as small-group teaching and literacy work stations for independent practice.

I didn't clean up the teachers' spaces, nor did we "trade spaces" and redo each other's rooms. We worked together, so teachers would have ownership for their spaces (much as we do with our students). It was a fresh start for us all. Later, Mrs. Fields told me it was the best investment she'd made in a long time, because all the teachers present applied the same techniques to their rooms as a result of their participation in the day. A new space can inspire new teaching ideas.

Over the years, I've helped many teachers redo their spaces—sometimes on a full scale, as at Mrs. Fields' school, and other times just a desk makeover. Every time, without fail, teachers feel they have a new start and are ready to look at teaching in a new light. Having an organized space can make more time for actual instruction and help teachers breathe as they try new ways of teaching.

This book contains examples from classrooms of brand-new teachers as well as those who have taught for over twenty years. We all have our own sets of challenges: limited storage space and growing class sizes; buildings in desperate need of remodeling; stuff "inherited" from the teacher who inhabited the room for the previous ten-plus years; new materials purchased with grant money but no space to store them; having to change grade levels and being afraid to let go of stuff we used for teaching in past years. No matter what the challenge, we must always make space for kids our priority. I believe that where there is a will, there is a way. We can and must make room for children.

Let's Get Started . . .

This book begins by looking at how to think about your teaching *and* your space before you move one piece of furniture. Chapter 1, "Planning Your Space," provides thought-provoking questions, helpful lists of what you might need, and tools to help you prioritize what you really want in your room. In Chapter 2, "Arranging Your Room," you'll find step-by-step instructions on how to set up your room that will save time and maximize space. Chapter 3, "Come On In!" explores the essential parts of classrooms, including the whole-group area, the small-group area, and the classroom library. This chapter also contains dozens of photos of literacy work stations in pre-K through fifth-grade classrooms to give you fresh, new ideas. It even looks at desks and tables and discusses how to organize them.

The fourth chapter, "Using Your Walls," examines what, how, and why we display and includes extensive information about word walls. In Chapter 5, "Organizing Your Stuff," we visit three classrooms to see how these teachers learned to pack up their things at the end of the year (while teaching until the last day of school), how to prepare for a move, and how to organize shelves and storage cabinets.

You'll notice that every chapter ends with Next Steps/Things to Try. Use these suggestions to help you put into action the thoughts and ideas you get as you read. Many suggestions include activities to try with a friend or colleague. I've found that it's much easier to do something with a partner than to go it alone. There is also a Continuum, so you can see where you currently are and what you can try along the way to get to your end goal.

As you read you may wonder where to get the materials being used in these classrooms. The Resources section at the back of the book, and especially the section "Where to Find It," will help you locate materials pictured in the photos without interrupting the flow of your reading and thinking.

You'll also come across many charts and tools to help you plan your space and your teaching and guide your thinking along the way. Reproducible forms of each planning chart can also be found in the "Resources" section.

Take a field trip with me to some of the classrooms I've visited over the past few years. I've been walking around, camera in hand, snapping photos and documenting space challenges and solutions. Some pictures are from classrooms I've spent only a few minutes in; others record change in one room over time. They were taken in all kinds of classrooms in urban, rural, and suburban settings. In portables, in rooms with no windows, and in small rooms. I live in Houston, and several were shot in that area. Houston is a relatively new, and expanding, city, so many of our schools are quite new, but the classrooms aren't necessarily large. However, all rooms seem bigger when they aren't full of stuff. So while you may not see your very own room reflected here, think about how you can adapt what you see to make it your own.

Teachers are creative people . . . we have to be. May this book inspire you to try some new things in your classroom, both with your space and, ultimately, your teaching. As A. A. Milne said, "Organizing is what you do before you do something, so that when you do it, it's not all mixed up." Embracing organization supports effective instruction and helps make classrooms places where children are valued.

Note to Administrators

Administrators can lead the way to helping teachers create pleasing environments conducive to teaching and learning. Teachers often rely on administrators to provide support as they make changes. They may need materials, such as storage containers or bookshelves; they may need help with getting rid of things; they may even ask for classroom makeovers!

In my work as a literacy coach, I found we were often scrambling to put together engaging, viable ideas for ongoing staff development. I was in charge of our PGO (Professional Growth Opportunities) time daily; every day a different grade level met for embedded staff development during the day. It was an awesome way to support teachers and their growth, but it was a challenge to keep it going.

Based on my experience directly helping dozens of schools improve their learning environments, and ultimately their teaching, I've outlined ten possible plans for professional development using this book. You'll find these in "Resources—Staff Development Suggestions." I hope you'll use these as a springboard and feel free to expand from there. Opportunities for teachers to think and talk together are rare; teachers will appreciate it if those times are well thought-out. May you find this book a resource and a support to improving instruction for the children you serve.

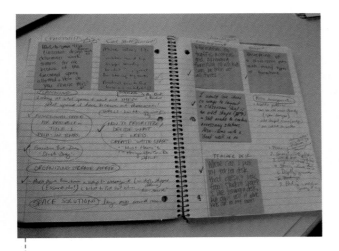 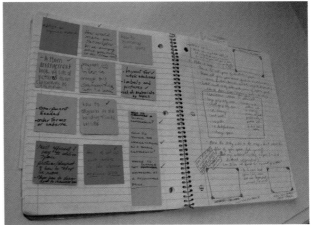

Figure I.1

These pages from my writer's notebook contain sticky notes from teachers with requests of what to include in my book. I also jot down notes and ideas here.

Thoughts About Classroom Space

- Classroom space impacts everything: instruction, behavior, and our (children's and teachers') sense of well-being.
- Improving classroom space can improve our teaching, help us manage our classrooms better, and help us all enjoy being in our rooms.
- A well-organized classroom that provides student ownership can teach students to be more independent.
- Cleaning up clutter can provide more space for kids.
- We don't need lots of "stuff" to teach well. Be thoughtful about what we purchase and store in our rooms. Develop things *with* our children that can be sent home during and at the end of the year.
- Rearranging our room to support instruction can bring about a change in our teaching. It can make way for including our students in taking ownership for their learning.

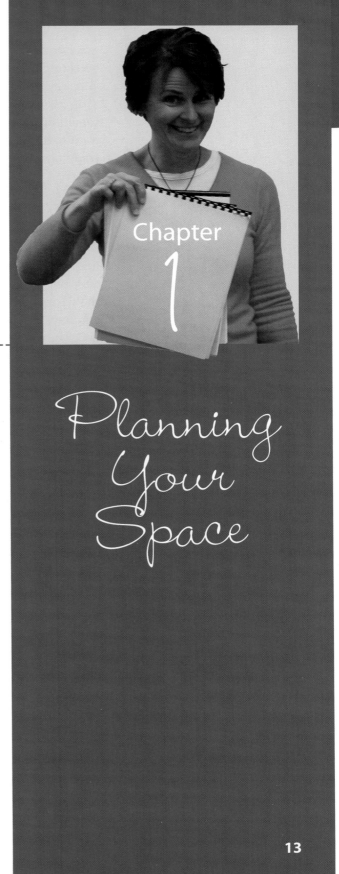

Chapter

1

Planning Your Space

When I used to set up my classroom, I'd move a desk here and a table there and then step back to see if I liked it. It took hours and usually didn't produce the results I'd hoped for. Only when I worked as a literacy coach and helped other teachers set up their rooms did I realize that creating a plan on paper *first* was a more efficient and effective way to arrange a classroom.

One day, my friend Pam, a second-grade teacher, called and asked for help with her room setup. She knew I'd been trying out ideas to help teachers organize their space. "You know how I always stay at school until 7 p.m.? I realize it's partly because many times I can't find my stuff, and it takes me forever to get things done. Could you help me reorganize my room?" And I'd thought she was just overdedicated!

Soon after, we met in her classroom and began a map of her space. As we worked, I asked her what was working for her and what she wanted to change. During our conversation, I noticed that she was having difficulty thinking about her room in a new way. She had been teaching in this space for several years and was used to it a certain way (even though parts weren't working for her). Finally I said, "You asked for help, but you don't seem ready. Every time I suggest something, you give an excuse why we can't do that. Are you sure you want to do this?" She took a deep breath and said, "Let's try again. I'm ready now." Change is hard—even when you want to try something new.

Together, we devised a plan for her room and *then* moved furniture. We redid her teacher work space and organized her small-group materials. We added new fabric chair covers (to brighten up and unify the space) and table skirts (to create additional storage), which gave her room a whole new look. She loved it and called me several days after the room redo. "Guess what happened today?" she said. "I put the scissors on a table, and I swear they spoke to me . . . 'I am scissors and have a home . . . put me where I belong.'" We had labeled all her desk items so it would be easier for her to put them away. It worked, and she began leaving school at a decent hour. As an added bonus, it provided a good model for her students. Years later, when visiting Pam at a different school, her room was well organized and working beautifully, and she told me she was helping other teachers with their room setups, too.

This chapter outlines step-by-step processes and tools to help you set up your room thoughtfully. It includes a system I've used in hundreds of classrooms like Pam's, with excellent results each time. It's helpful to find a friend to assist you with room setup, someone who is good with space and can look at your room in a new light. If you've taught in the same room for a number of years, it's sometimes difficult to arrange it any other way than how you've always done it. Take a step back, rethink your room using this book for inspiration, and make a plan before you move anything.

Planning Your Space

Think about your instruction first . . . then plan for space to make that happen.

- *Do you ever find yourself moving furniture around at the end of a challenging day with your kids, hoping it will improve behavior tomorrow?*
- *Is your desk strewn with papers and projects?*
- *Would you like more space and better organization in your classroom?*

If so, then this book is for you!

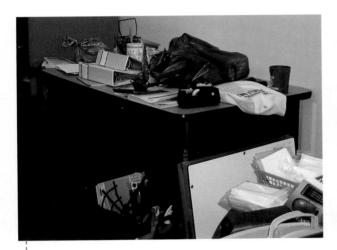

Pam's Teacher Desk Before

Pam's teacher desk was a "clutter magnet." She used it primarily as a catchall. She decided she'd like to get rid of it and use her small-group teaching area as a teacher desk area as well.

There is a direct link between structure, organization, and effective instruction.

Clutter can lead to chaos.

Pam's Teacher Desk Gone . . . Teacher Work Space After

We used a square table that doubles as a small-group teaching area and her "teacher desk." We placed a shelf to the right of the filing cabinet to organize her small-group teaching materials. On top of the shelf is a drawer organizer that holds desk supplies. We also attached a magnetic holder to the top right of the filing cabinet and labeled it to hold things like her scissors, pencils, stamps, etc. The black file boxes hold little books for guided reading groups. Phonics charts and a character feelings chart are posted on the wall for reference during small-group reading instruction. Blue and white baskets on the floor hold projects she's working on.

Begin with the End in Mind . . .

Start the year by planning for space BEFORE you set up your classroom.

Step One: THINK about the teaching you want to do this year. Plan for spaces that match the way you want to teach.
- What do I want to be sure to include every day in my teaching?
- What spaces will I need to have in my classroom to make this happen?
- Where will this instruction take place? What materials will we need? Where will I keep them so I can work more efficiently and effectively? How can I promote student independence?

Classroom Spaces to Consider

- whole-group teaching area
- small-group teaching area
- classroom library
- word wall
- computers
- teacher desk/work area

- literacy work stations, such as listening, writing, Big Book, pocket chart, and portable stations
- student desks or tables
- math materials area
- storage spaces

MY INSTRUCTION	SPACE I'LL NEED	THOUGHTS ON SETTING UP
more modeling in whole group	• whole-group teaching area	• place near the board where I can chart things • large rug to define the space • place to keep books and writing stuff I'm teaching with
daily small-group instruction	• small-group teaching area	• have a clear view of all stations so I can see what rest of the class is doing • put near a bulletin board so I can display anchor charts • put shelves and baskets there to hold small-group materials—everything at my fingertips
more one-on-one reading and writing conferences	• student desks grouped in 4s or 5s	• need rolling chair, clipboard with note cards, file box to keep track of notes • keep in my teacher's desk area
writer's workshop	• whole-group teaching area • student desks grouped in 4s or 5s	• large writing easel at front of room • place to keep writing folders in file boxes, possibly near the writing station so kids can work with them there for extra practice • status of the class board

Step Two:
THINK about your *ideal* classroom.
- What does your *ideal* room look like?
- Your desk or work space?
- The kids' desks or tables?
- Your storage spaces?
- Your teaching areas?

Mark photos in this book and have conversations with your colleagues to help you dream.

Step Three:
Now LOOK around.
- How do you feel when you enter your classroom?
- How do the children feel when they come in your room?
- Does the entranceway to your classroom feel open and inviting?
- What do you need in terms of furniture, open space, and learning areas?
- Ask your students for their input, too.

Third-Grade Entrance Before

This teacher had too much stuff in her entryway, including a Big Book stand, a file cabinet, and even an empty book rounder. When you entered the room, you saw clutter. It wasn't a welcoming space.

Third-Grade Entrance After

We moved furniture and opened up the entry to feel more inviting. Now, clearly defined spaces, such as the classroom library along the far wall, are visible. There is room for children.

Have nothing in your classroom "that you do not know to be useful, or believe to be beautiful."
—adapted from William Morris

Inviting Entrance . . . Outside the Classroom

This display is for parents. The flower cutouts list items parents might donate to the classroom. On the small table are projects for parents to help with. The bench is for parents to sit on while waiting after school or for conferences.

*Mapping Tip: Decide where to put desks **last**, not first . . . you'll see more possibilities for using the perimeters without the desks in the way and better utilize your space.*

Traffic Patterns . . .

- Be sure to have spaces where students can walk (not run) from place to place in the classroom. Walk through to see if you bump into any furniture.
- Create spaces to walk between tables to facilitate while kids are working there.
- Make a clear path to/from whole-group and small-group teaching areas.
- Beware of "dead space"—areas not being utilized to the fullest. These are often found in the middle of the room or near desks.
- Don't create a "runway" to your library (a long, open space where kids can run) that ends in a pile of pillows in the middle of this space.

Step Four: Make a map. (See Chapter 2, "Arranging Your Room," for more ideas.)
- Use a 12-by-18-inch piece of construction paper.
- Draw all your permanent fixtures on it (windows, doors, bulletin boards, outlets, computer drops, built-ins, etc.).
- Label small sticky notes with names of spaces you'd like to have on each. Refer to chart on pages 22–23. One name per sticky note.
- Place the sticky notes on the map and think about the flow of your space.
  Ask yourself:
  - Does my entrance feel inviting and open (or is it cluttered with furniture)?
  - Can I see all spaces from my small-group table?
  - Do I have dead space (big areas that are unused or cluttered, like corners or spaces behind my desk)?
- Take inventory of what you've got, one bit at a time.

Don't Move **Any** Furniture Until Your Map Is Done! Move sticky notes, not furniture, and save yourself about 8 hours of backbreaking labor.

"The difference between a dream and a goal is a plan."
—Anonymous

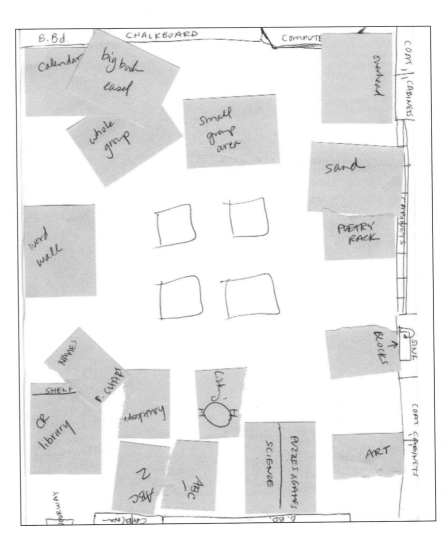

Be Wise When Planning for Furniture in Your Classroom

"The amount of space you have cannot be changed— the amount of stuff you have can."

—Peter Walsh

Ask Yourself:

- Do I really need all that furniture? Use the chart on the next page to take inventory of what you've got.
- What can I get double-duty from? (see Chapter 2,"Arranging Your Room")—small-group table doubles as a teacher desk; file cabinet stores paper and is a word study work station using magnetic letters
- Is that piece of furniture a clutter magnet?
- How many file cabinets do I really need? (see Chapter 5, "Organizing Your Stuff")
- Do I use my cabinets, shelves, drawers, most effectively? (see Chapter 5, "Organizing Your Stuff")
- Where do I put paper as it comes in? (see Chapter 5, "Organizing Your Stuff")
- How am I sharing the space with my students?

"Help! I need more space!"

—any teacher, USA

Plan for kids to face you during small group, so they're not distracted by the rest of the class.

Consider How Your Space Will Help Kids Be Independent

- Put things where kids can reach them.
- Label EVERYTHING. Use pictures and words to help all students.
- You might get students to help make the labels.

-------- **MY FURNITURE INVENTORY** --------

WHAT I'VE GOT	PURPOSE IT SERVES	KEEP IT	GET RID OF IT
2 Big Book easels	should be holding Big Books while I'm modeling	move one to whole-group area	give other one to some-one else who needs it
large table in whole-group area	holding papers and books I might use this week	move to side wall and turn into station for writing and word study	
old box for holding out-of-adoption books	storing old books we no longer use		recycle the box and books
bookshelf that's falling apart	holding books by my desk, because it's not safe for kids		clear out cabinet space to store these; get rid of bookshelf
old, oversized display unit from card store I got for free 10 years ago	displaying books in library		too big—use a smaller shelf

MATERIALS RECOMMENDED FOR SETTING UP YOUR CLASSROOM

Note: Check on fire codes *before* using lamps, fabric, rugs, pillows, etc., in your room.

ESSENTIALS/MUST-HAVES	OTHER THINGS YOU MIGHT LIKE HERE	LINK TO INSTRUCTION
Whole-Group Teaching Area • large rug/carpet squares/mats to define large-group teaching area • Big Book easel/writing easel • overhead projector or document camera on cart • calendar area for math	**Whole-Group Teaching Area** • comfy teacher chair (if you have space) • laundry basket for Big Book storage • small shelves for storing teacher materials needed for the day	**Whole-Group Teaching Area** • modeling how to read, write (and learn math, science, and social studies) • read-aloud, shared reading, modeled and shared writing, calendar work, group discussions, sharing time
Small-Group Teaching Area • table for small-group teaching • shelves or clear plastic drawer units for small-group reading materials behind the table • place this by a bulletin board/display space (to post anchor charts)	**Small-Group Teaching Area** • 6 dry erase boards and markers • tabletop dry erase/magnetic easel • 6 sets of magnetic letters (lowercase) • plastic tackle box for storing magnetic letters • anchor charts (developed with kids)	**Small-Group Teaching Area** • supporting 4–6 kids at a time as readers, writers, thinkers, mathematicians in small-group instruction • small groups for reading, writing, or math; literature discussion group meetings
Classroom Library • bookshelves • plastic shoeboxes or baskets for books • labels for book baskets (made WITH kids)	**Classroom Library** • small rug to define the space • silk plants • comfy kid-size chairs/pillows • lamp • display space for anchor charts on book choice and related reading strategies and book reviews	**Classroom Library** • place to self-select books for independent reading • cozy area to read in during literacy work stations • place to practice what we've been learning about: genre, authors, content, strategies
Writing Area/Work Station • small table or two desks pushed together • trays for stacking and organizing paper • container for writing utensils	**Writing Area/Work Station** • writing supports (dictionaries, thesaurus, writing models) • student mailboxes • fun kid-size chairs • bulletin board nearby	**Writing Area/Work Station** • may be a place for materials to be stored for writer's workshop • space to practice writing during literacy work stations time
Other Literacy Stations • computers • ABC/word study • listening • Big Books • baskets or clear plastic containers for portable stations • "I Can" lists or directions written with students • management board	**Other Literacy Stations** • overhead, pocket chart, buddy reading, drama, poetry, etc. • materials to support above stations • tri-fold project boards (for portable stations) • storage unit for portable stations (wire cubes, milk crates, etc.)	**Other Literacy Stations** • places for students to practice reading and writing skills *previously taught* in whole group and/or small group

---------MATERIALS RECOMMENDED FOR SETTING UP YOUR CLASSROOM---------

Note: Check on fire codes *before* using lamps, fabric, rugs, pillows, etc., in your room.

ESSENTIALS/MUST-HAVES	OTHER THINGS YOU MIGHT LIKE HERE	LINK TO INSTRUCTION
Word Wall • cards with upper- and lowercase letters written on them (and picture cue for phonics in primary grades) • word wall words typed large enough (in black) for all students to see • low, interactive placement for students in pre-K, K, and grade 1 (so kids can see and reach words) • interesting words for vocabulary building in grades 2 and up • high-frequency words in pre-K through grade 1	**Word Wall** • shelves/stacking baskets for ABC/word study materials by the word wall • sorting space or large metal tray for sorts • place this near your ABC/word study station and your writing station, if possible, so kids can access these words	**Word Wall** • display for words we're paying attention to as readers and writers • make connections to these words while modeling how to read and write • use and spell these words correctly in your reading and writing throughout the day • in pre-K to grade 1, be able to take words on/off wall as you need them or want to explore them and how they relate to other words
Math Area • shelves and containers for math manipulatives • large wall for displaying math information	**Math Area** • plastic containers with labels for math manipulatives	**Math Area** • place to store math materials used for instruction and math stations for independent practice
Social Studies, Science Area • globes, maps • science manipulatives stored in containers by unit of study • book display area for unit of study	**Social Studies, Science Area** • open-faced book shelves (to display books for current unit of study) • microscopes, other lab materials	**Social Studies, Science Area** • place to store materials used for teaching science and social studies • may be used as a station to practice what was previously taught
Desks/Tables • student desks grouped together to save space (groups of 4–6) • teacher desk in small, out-of-the-way space (to maximize room for kids' learning)	**Desks/Tables** • might get rid of teacher desk and use small-group teaching table as desk, too (or use desk for double duty) • use small computer table as teacher desk	**Desks/Tables** • places for students to work independently to practice reading, writing, math, science, social studies, etc. • personal spaces for kids and for teacher

Furniture List

Needed for Classroom of 25 Children (provided by school):

- 2–3 small tables
  - one for small-group instruction (with 6 kid-size chairs)
  - one for writing station
- 2–3 rugs to define spaces
  - large one for whole-group teaching area
  - smaller one for classroom library
- 25–27 student desks (or 5 tables) with student chairs
- 1 teacher desk (or small computer table to serve as teacher desk)
- 2 teacher chairs (with wheels preferably)
  - one for teacher desk area
  - one for small-group instruction area
- 1 two-sided Big Book/writing easel (one side used for teaching with Big Books and other side for modeling writing)
  - preferably dry erase/magnetic surface
  - large enough to accommodate Big Books and chart tablets

- 5–6 small bookshelves (could be built in or freestanding)
  - two to three for classroom library
  - two for math manipulatives
  - one for other storage
- 1 overhead projector or document camera
- 4–6 computers for students to use
- cabinets for storage of teaching supplies
- cubbies for student storage of coats, backpacks, lunch boxes, etc.
- 3–4 pocket charts
- 1–2 tape recorders
- 2 file cabinets (shorter ones preferred)

THINGS YOU MIGHT BE ABLE TO LIVE WITHOUT

ITEM	WHY YOU DON'T NEED THIS	WHAT TO DO INSTEAD
junk tables	places to stack stuff that has no home	find a home for everything you keep—label it and put it away
extra desk for instructional aide	aides shouldn't be sitting at desks	aides should help teach or monitor, not sit
large teacher desk	takes up valuable classroom space and becomes stacking area	have small-group table double as teacher desk; or use smaller desk/computer work space
extra furniture	somebody gave it to me and I might use it someday	get rid of it—put it in storage or throw it away (if old and beat up)
stacks of construction paper	every year kids bring this to school and I have too much of it	give it away to needy school or families
stuff hanging from the ceilings	it can be distracting to ADHD or autistic kids	use wall space for display instead—be selective in what you display
microwave/refrigerator	takes up valuable classroom space	eat lunch in the faculty room—it might do you good to get out of your classroom for a bit
big boxes that instructional materials often come in	they're often unsightly, large, and take up lots of room	get rid of them unless you are required to keep them—use smaller storage containers to store materials you received

Special Items for Pre-K and Kindergarten Classrooms

- blocks and shelves for storing them
- housekeeping/dramatic play materials—kitchen, plastic food, pots and pans, etc.
- sand/water table
- science table
- Lego table
- painting easel (1 or 2)
- tables no higher than 20 inches
- shelves no higher than 30 inches

Blocks area in pre-K to K includes carpet for building, labeled spaces for storage, and Lego table.

Sand/water table in pre-K to K is topped with piece of dry erase shower board that doubles as a projection space for the overhead work station when removed.

Kitchen furniture is set up to encourage dramatic play and oral language development in pre-K to K classrooms.

Planning for Dual-Language Classrooms

- You might have signs, displays, and directions in Spanish in one color (such as blue) and the same in English in another color (such as green).
- Consider having two sections of your classroom library. One set of shelves might house Spanish books and another English. Label each to match.
- Hang two pocket charts back-to-back. Or display two side by side. Place English words and sentences on one side and Spanish on the other, so kids can practice activities in either language. Again, color-code them to match that language.

Spanish books are easily accessible in one part of a bilingual classroom library.

This library is from the same classroom, with English books in labeled baskets.

This writing station in a bilingual classroom has an "I Can" list in Spanish on one side and English on the other side to help children remember what to practice at this station. Students helped to create these lists *with* their teacher.

Planning for Special Needs Students

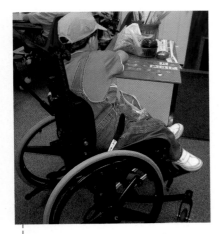

The ABC station is at a table, so a child in a wheelchair can easily access it.

- If you have a child in a wheelchair, you'll need to make space for the chair to fit through aisles. Walk around the room with the child and ask for his input on how easy it is to move through the space. Adjust your room as needed. The student will feel included and will be able to function more independently.
- For whole-group time, think about where the child will sit to feel included and be able to see what you're modeling.
- During small-group time, be sure the wheelchair will fit at your table. Adjust the table and student chair heights as needed.
- When planning for literacy work stations, be sure to set these up so the child feels included. For example, at the writing station, provide clipboards and a chair for another student to be seated at eye level with a partner in a wheelchair to facilitate easy conversation. Be sure your classroom library has a place where the child's chair will fit.
- When setting up individual desks or tables, you might seat a child in a wheelchair at the end of a table for her to have easier access to this space.
- If a child has special equipment, like step stools or a stander, provide a place to store this so it's accessible to you and the child.
- Think about where an extra adult will sit if he accompanies a special needs student per an IEP.

Two boys read together at a Big Book station. There is plenty of space for a wheelchair to get to this area in the whole-group teaching area.

Space is available beside the teacher in this small-group area, so there is easy access for a wheelchair to fit there. The table height matches the students in chairs and the wheelchair.

Planning If You Have No Walls (Open Classrooms)

- Use specially designed furniture (often on wheels) as dividers.
- Space is often limited in these rooms, so use minimal furniture. Make sure what you use can do double-duty whenever possible.
- Have your word wall on a portable chalkboard.
- Use more portable stations than stationary ones, if needed. Tri-fold project boards, like those used for science fair, can be folded up and put away when not in use.

Classroom library is carved out in an open classroom by creating a "corner" with two small bookshelves. A portable bulletin board creates a "wall" along the back.

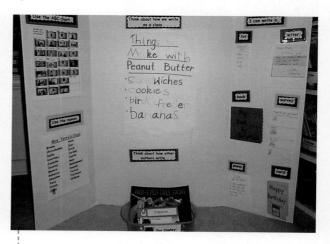

Tri-fold boards are used to create a backdrop for a portable writing station (top photo) and drama station (bottom photo). The teacher posts "help" for writing on the board during whole-group instruction. Then kids practice with this at the writing station.

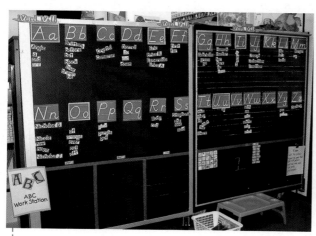

Portable magnetic chalkboard on wheels is a divider between two classrooms and doubles as an interactive word wall and an ABC/word study station.

The drama station has an "I Can" list (written with students) and a dry erase surface for writing. Kids stand behind it to dramatize stories and read reader's theater scripts. They use it like a stage.

Planning for Portable Buildings

- Lack of storage calls for creative solutions. Use all "wasted" spaces, as shown below.
- Cover table fronts and sides with fabric attached with Velcro to provide extra storage space underneath.
- Bulletin boards are movable. Ask your custodian for help in moving them to more conducive areas.
- Use fabric at windows to brighten up space. Add plants, too, to add life to the room.
- Plan for only one whole-group area. Don't use too much furniture. Space is usually limited!

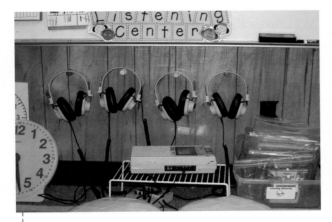

This photo shows a close-up of the listening station under the dry erase board in the whole-group teaching area.

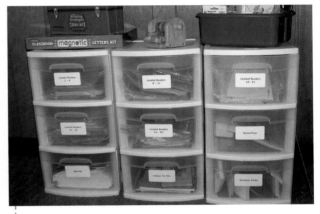

Plastic stacking drawers provide storage in the small-group teaching area behind the small-group table.

A custodian moves a pegboard to the writing station for storage and display of things to help kids practice writing here. Note the skirted table that provides extra storage space.

Whole-group teaching area is brightened up with an area rug. Dry erase board, Big Book easel, and writing easel all serve dual purposes during whole group and at stations practice. Note listening stations in the low space under the dry erase board.

Planning for New Technology

- Interactive whiteboards or Smart Boards are wonderful but take up a lot of room when not mounted. Mount them to a wall whenever possible.
- If it's on a stand, try placing your interactive whiteboard in a corner at an angle. Surprisingly, it often gives the illusion of taking up less space.
- Extra computer jacks may be added to your classroom. Think carefully about their placement if given this opportunity for input.
- Be careful about where you place your computer if it's on a stand. Be sure it doesn't block students' view. Sit at a variety of spaces in your class and make your eye level match where your kids' will be. Adjust the computer stand as needed. Be sure to place computers where they won't distract other kids working on their own or in your small group.

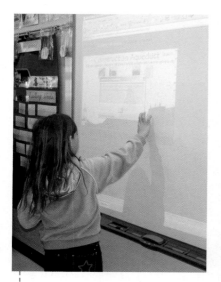

Students practice with the interactive whiteboard that is mounted on the wall during literacy work stations.

Use desktop computers as stationary stations and laptops as portable stations.

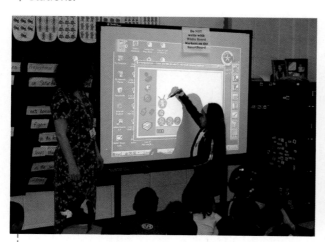

Teach with your interactive whiteboard in whole-group instruction. Model well and be explicit about how to use this piece of equipment, so kids will be able to use it independently during literacy stations.

Make an "Instead Box" *with* your students. Ask them to help think of things you could put here that they could do independently in case technology-related stations, such as listening or computer, aren't working properly.

Planning for a Teacher Desk

Ask Yourself: "Do I Want a Teacher Desk?"

1. Is my desk a place where I rarely sit but use it for stacking lots of papers?
2. Do I find myself sitting at a clean table to do work after school instead of at my desk?
3. Is my desk taking up lots of space in my room?

If you answered YES to questions 1 to 3, you might want to get rid of your teacher desk.

4. Does my school require that a teacher desk remain in my classroom?
5. Do I like my teacher desk and keep it organized?
6. Is my desk a lovely space I can call my own?

If you answered YES to questions 4 to 6, keep your teacher desk.

Here are some ideas for planning for your teacher space (teacher desk or alternative):

- Place your teacher desk area away from the entrance and your flow of traffic.
- Don't use the best corner in the room for your teacher space. Share with your students. (It often makes a great library area!)
- Plan for your teacher desk area to be near cabinets or shelves for storing your stuff.
- Put a calendar and display board by your teacher area (for posting notes and reminders).
- Provide a space for everything important that will need to be handled here. (For more ideas, see the "Teacher Desk/Work Space" section in Chapter 3, "Come On In!")

This desk has become a clutter magnet.

A traditional teacher desk doesn't have to take up lots of space.

The front of this third-grade teacher's desk is turned into a poetry work station and is positioned at a 90-degree angle beside a heating element. Magnetic words from a kit bought from www.magneticpoetry.com are on the desk front. Other poetry materials are stored in front of the desk.

Two students use a corner of the top of the teacher's desk as a writing station. The desk is portioned off with red masking tape to show the students' section.

Be Brave at the Start of the Year

On your bulletin boards post signs saying, "UNDER CONSTRUCTION. COMING SOON . . . KIDS' WORK"

When children enter your room, what do they think?

· The teacher wants my ideas in here. It's OUR room.

· The teacher has already set up everything. This is my TEACHER'S room.

Don't "decorate" your classroom. Instead, plan for instruction and leave some room for your students!

- Design an attractive, inviting space for your kids at the beginning of the school year. But don't overdo it.
- Choose 2–3 colors to use in your room. This ties your space together and can even create the illusion of more room.
- If you choose to use fabric for bulletin boards and curtains, use the same fabric from space to space. Match them to the colors you're using in your room. Use fire-retardant fabric if needed. **Check fire codes before using fabric.**
- Don't cover up every space on the walls. Leave room for things you'll create *with* your kids! Cover bulletin boards and put up borders. But don't plaster the boards with premade stuff.

Thoughts on Using Color in Your Room

- Choose 2 or 3 basic colors that coordinate.
- Consider effects these colors may have on your children. Blue and green are calming colors. Red and orange evoke excitement and stimulate appetite.
- Don't just throw things together. Have a plan.
- Keep it simple.
- Use calming colors and prints/solids.

Here are some color scheme suggestions:

Sophisticated color scheme (for older kids)

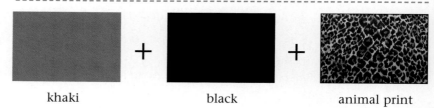

khaki　　　　　　　　　black　　　　　　　　animal print

Calming color scheme

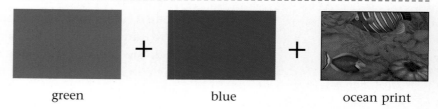

green　　　　　　　　　blue　　　　　　　　ocean print

Cheerful color scheme

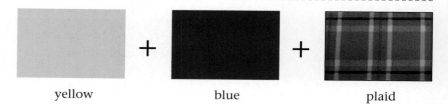

yellow　　　　　　　　blue　　　　　　　　　plaid

My color scheme is:

Next Steps/Things to Try

1. Think about your teaching priorities. Look at your space. Do you have room for the things you most value? Can you easily find what you need at your fingertips while teaching? You might fill out the My Instruction/Space I'll Need/Thoughts on Setting Up chart on page 199. Compare ideas and charts with your teaching team.

2. Ask a friend to stand in your entryway and give an honest opinion. Is it open and inviting? Likewise, ask him to sit at your small-group table and look around the room. Are all spaces easily seen? Work together to move anything that might be hindering your views.

3. Map out your classroom on paper with a friend (before moving any furniture). Use the sticky-note process described in this section. Plan your space with instruction in mind. Be sure to have an adequate space for whole-group instruction where everything you need is within your reach. Then work together to move furniture to maximize your space.

4. What purpose is your teacher desk serving? Try ideas from this book to better utilize this space. Perhaps you can make it serve dual purposes. See the "Teacher Desk/Work Space" section in Chapter 3 for ideas on making your desk more user-friendly.

5. What is your room's color scheme? How does it make you feel? What effect do you think it's having on your students? You might browse through this book to look for color schemes that appeal to you. Or find a fabric sample that coordinates nicely with your room and use that for inspiration. Remember to limit it to 2 or 3 colors.

6. Where are you on this continuum for planning your space? Think about next steps you'd like to take.

1   2   3   4

1. Just happy to have my room set up. Put things where they seem to fit. Using all kinds of colors. I might have too much furniture, and I might not have enough.

2. Realizing some areas of my room aren't well planned. Some areas get cluttered. Not sure what to do with it, though.

3. My room needs some reorganization. I'm going to choose one area and use ideas from this chapter to tackle it.

4. I'm working with a friend to reevaluate my entryway and how my whole space works for instruction. We are going to work together to make a map. First, I'm jotting down what's important to me. I'm making a thoughtful plan for space.

Chapter 2

Arranging Your Room

Patty, a friend who teaches first grade, called me late in the summer. "I've decided to change schools and am moving to a new district and a brand-new space. Will you be able to help me set up my classroom?" Due to prior scheduling, I was unable to go with her to her new classroom. But I had an idea.

"Do you know what your space looks like? Can you come over to my house for about an hour? It's all the time I've got, but I think maybe I can help," I suggested. While she drove to my home, I assembled the tools we'd need—sticky notes, blank paper, and some markers. Simple stuff.

When Patty arrived, we talked about her priorities. What did she want to include in her new room? What were her nonnegotiables? We'd been working together five or six years, and I'd helped her set up several classrooms since I'd been her literacy coach. I knew what she had and the feel she wanted in her room. We began by taking a large piece of plain construction paper and mapping out all the things that couldn't be moved along the perimeter (bulletin boards, electric outlets, the doorway, and the all-important computer drops). Next, we jotted down names of spaces she wanted to have on sticky notes: classroom library, large-group teaching area, small-group teaching area, literacy work stations (computer, Big Book, pocket chart, buddy reading, etc.), and a math area. Then we moved the sticky notes around the paper until we found a workable arrangement. The whole time we worked, we talked about the placement.

"I want the whole-group area here by the chalkboard. I'll want to use the board to display charts and write down our schedule."

"Let's put the small-group teaching area back here. You'll be able to see the whole classroom from this space. We don't want any hidden spaces where we can't see kids."

"What about a corner for the classroom library? This is the only workable one I see. Let's place the tall bookshelf in the corner and angle it to invite the kids in."

"I have some stacking baskets we can use for portable stations. Let's put those by a bulletin board. We can hang a pocket chart there and make that a pocket chart station."

"I'll need a large rug to anchor the whole-group teaching area. This room needs some color to liven it up. I saw some carpets at a hardware store. I'll need to measure the space to be sure I get the right size before I go shopping."

When we finished the classroom mapping, Patty thanked me and exclaimed, "You just saved me about eight hours of backbreaking furniture-moving. That was the easiest setup we ever did together!" She went on her way and moved the furniture several days later.

The following year, I photographed the setup of her room at the start of the year and refined my thinking about prioritizing—what to place first, second, and third. I always put instruction first as we made decisions. Amazingly, after setting up the room, Patty didn't change it throughout the year. A thoughtful plan and arrangement paid off in running a well-managed classroom. In fact, a year later I videotaped in Patty's room and created the series *Launching Literacy Stations* to help others learn how to teach literacy in a thoughtful, highly engaging way.

The system you'll read about on the following pages was created over the years. It's helped me whenever I've worked around space challenges, such as portable buildings or classrooms with odd configurations. In this chapter, you'll see how we used it to set up a relatively small space (a 25-by-27-foot room for 22 to 24 students) and to revitalize an old science lab that was turned into a regular third-grade classroom in an inner-city school. This step-by-step process works in all kinds of rooms and across all grade levels. Use it as a guide to help you arrange your room. Then step back and enjoy teaching in your new space.

Classroom Management Begins with Room Arrangement

· You've got a plan.
· Grab a friend and set up that classroom!
· Keep in mind . . . traffic flow and closing up "dead space."

You can head off many problems at the pass with thoughtful planning of space. Here's a step-by-step plan for setting up your room that is guaranteed to save you time and space:
  Use your plan.

• *Start with your planning map. (See Chapter 1, "Planning Your Space," for ideas.)*

• *Then work with a friend to move furniture and put things in place, step by step.*

Planning Map for Classroom

This map matches the classroom setup that follows in Patty's first-grade classroom, a 25-by-27-foot room for 24 children.

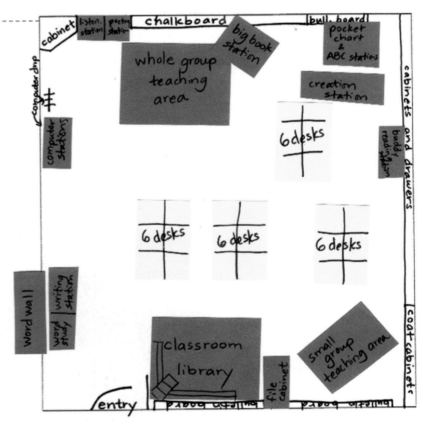

"I used to set up the desks first. Now I set up the desks LAST! I spend most of my time teaching in whole group the first few weeks of school. And kids pay better attention when gathered close to me in the whole-group teaching area."

—first-grade teacher

Patty's desks are stacked in the middle of room before setting up. We kept them out of the way so we could see the perimeter and be able to use all her space effectively!

Step One:

Just put out the big stuff first. And remember . . . desks last!!!

Set up your whole-group teaching area.

- Put it near a large wall space and/or chalkboard or dry erase board so you'll have a place to write and display charts. If the board is magnetic, it's even better, since you can use magnets to attach things!
- Use a large rug to define the whole-group space and bring kids up close to increase their attention and engagement.
- Put your Big Book easel or writing easel here for shared reading and writing modeling.

| Step Two: | Next, arrange your small-group teaching area. |

- Try to put it near a wall or bulletin board so you can display anchor charts developed *with* your kids here. (See Chapter 4, "Using Your Walls," for ideas on anchor charts.)
- Place shelves or stacking drawers behind your table for storage of materials to increase your time-on-task with kids.
- A file cabinet nearby makes a magnetic surface for word work in small group.

| Step Three: | Then, set up your classroom library. |

- Use a corner if you've got one to create a welcoming space. Angle shelves to invite children in to read.
- Low bookshelves allow children to easily access books they want to read.
- Anchor the area with a small rug to define the space.
- Make it cozy with a couple of comfy chairs and a lamp.
- Use a silk plant or flowers to breathe life into this space.
- Don't put out any books yet. The kids can help you with this during the first week of school.

The file cabinet doesn't need to go in a corner. Here it's used to separate small group from the classroom library.

Step Four:

Hang up your word wall.

- If possible, place this near your whole-group teaching area so you can teach with it.
- Make the word wall low and interactive in pre-K, K, and grade 1 so kids can reach and manipulate the words.
- Use magnetic strips or Velcro to make the word wall interactive.
- Hang words as you teach with them.
- Start with kids' names at the first of the year, since a child's name is usually the first word he learns to read and write.
- You might hang phonics cards to easily create your word wall, as shown.

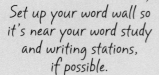

Set up your word wall so it's near your word study and writing stations, if possible.

This six-foot-long table will be divided in half to make room for a word study station on the left and a writing station on the right.

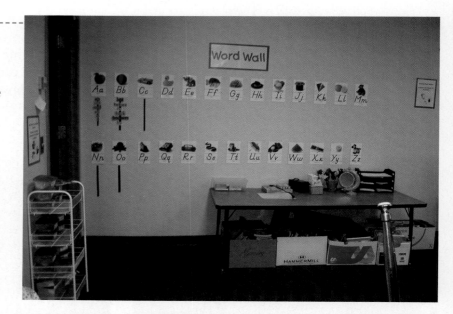

Table legs are lowered with an Allen wrench to give more space for the word wall and keep it accessible to students. Add a fabric skirt with Velcro and create an instant storage space under the table.

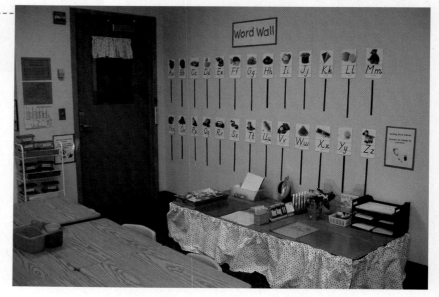

| **Step Five:** | If you plan to use work stations, set them up around the perimeter of your room. |

- Some stations are stationary, like the pocket chart station in the right corner of the top photo, to utilize existing space. A pocket chart is tacked low onto a bulletin board, so kids can easily reach it.
- The Big Book station is now in place, too.
- Several portable stations are in this corner, including ABC/word study stations in portable baskets and the creation station with art materials housed on low, open shelves. Kids carry these materials to desks to work independently.
- In the front left corner of the classroom, the listening station materials are placed on the floor in a portable basket, as shown in the bottom photo. The poetry station is set up on the chart stand along with an open basket that holds other poetry materials.
- The computer station is to the left. Make everything easy for kids to reach independent of the teacher.

Step Six:

You could also use your computers as a computer station.

- Place computers on kidney-shaped tables or trapezoid-shaped tables (rather than long rectangular tables) to save wall space here.
- If possible, try not to put all computers on a long table against a wall. It wastes too much wall space.
- Using flat-screen monitors and/or laptops (if available) will also save space.

Step Seven:

Place student desks in the middle of the room in the space that remains.

- Put desks in groups of four, five, or six to maximize space.
- This arrangement also encourages student collaboration when doing group work.
- Desks can always be separated, as needed.
- Be sure all students can see the front of the room if you model by your chalkboard or dry erase board.

Step Eight: Set up your teacher desk LAST!

This teacher uses her small-group teaching area as a desk, too. Her teacher desk took up too much space in her tiny classroom, so she got rid of it (with permission). Now she is using this space for "double duty." Her teacher stuff is stored in the cupboard to the left and the file cabinet to the right.

You might use "furniture movers" when moving big or heavy furniture. Slide them under the legs or corners of bulky items. You can buy these at home building stores, such as Home Depot and Lowe's.

For more information on setting up a teacher desk, see the section "Desks/Tables" in Chapter 3, "Come On In!"

Desk Arrangement Gives Kids a Message

Traditional Classroom

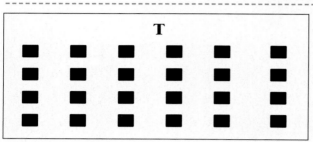

Teacher:

"I am the teacher. You will do as I say. I have all the answers. Listen to me. I don't want you sitting near each other, because then you'll talk and won't listen to me. I'm watching you all the time. "

Students:

"We are supposed to do what the teacher says. There is one way to do things . . . the teacher's way."

Connected Rows

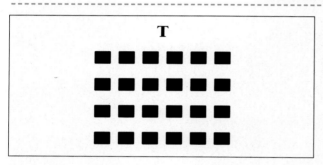

Teacher:

"I have the information. I want you to be part of my group, but I'm not ready for you to be on your own. I want to see all of you with your books open, listening and following along. I'll hand out papers and you can pass them down your row."

Students:

"Watch the teacher. He will show us what to do. Stay in your seats. That's where you do your work."

Horseshoe

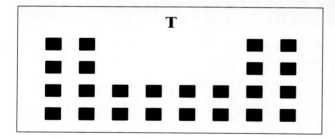

Teacher:

"We will work together to learn. We will have discussions in here. I'm not going to be the only one thinking. I'm interested in what you have to say. "

Students:

"We are going to be expected to think and participate. The teacher will lead our discussions. We will work together."

Table Groups

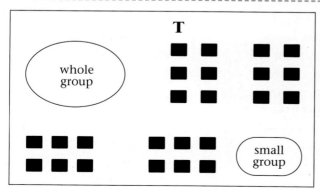

Teacher:

"We will be learning together in lots of ways. Sometimes we'll meet on the floor as a group to learn. Other times we'll sit with a few of you at a time to learn together. You'll sit at your tables sometimes and work together, too.

Students:

"We are all learners and will work together. My ideas are valued here and will be used to help others. My teacher cares about what I think and will use that to help me learn."

Before and After Photos of a Third-Grade Classroom at the Start of the School Year

This room was designed to be a science lab, but is now a regular classroom in an urban school. The teacher attended training on how to organize a classroom before we began. We helped to fine-tune the process in the makeover photos shown on the following pages.

Whole-Group Teaching Area BEFORE

There is a space to gather students in the front of the room, but the title floor is cold and uninviting.

Whole-Group Teaching Area AFTER

- A rug has been added to define the space and add interest to the room.
- A Big Book easel (found in the back of the classroom) was moved to the front to use during shared reading of nonfiction Big Books during whole-group instruction.
- Storage shelves were moved to the front of the room for the teacher to keep materials used during whole-group instruction.

Small-Group Teaching Area BEFORE

Small-group table is placed in front of the science lab table in the middle of the room.

Small-Group Teaching Area AFTER

- Round table for small group was moved to a corner where it took up less space and was closer to shelves for storing small-group teaching materials.
- Anchor charts can be displayed on cabinet doors and accessed during small-group time.
- The word wall is nearby for drawing attention to new vocabulary while reading in small group.

Classroom Library
BEFORE

- There are pillows here, but no books.
- Every bulletin board in the room is a different color, which adds to visual distraction.
- Teacher supply store charts and pictures add to the wall clutter.

Classroom Library
AFTER

- Wooden bookshelf moved from back of room to under the TV to anchor the new classroom library and attractively display books.
- Inexpensive plastic shelves added to house books.
- Dollar store baskets in yellow, blue, and green added to organize books and create a calming atmosphere.
- Silk plant breathes life into the space.
- Comfortable seating and a small rug (from back of room) invite children in to enjoy a book.
- Things removed from wall and bulletin boards changed to coordinate and calm.

Now we have an inviting space where we can add classroom library books.

Word Wall and Writing Station BEFORE

- Note the large chalkboard and science table covered in black metallic contact paper.
- Note the cursive alphabet frieze above the word wall.

Word Wall and Writing Station AFTER

- After removing contact paper from chalkboard, it is now "sticky" and words can be easily put on/off the wall.
- Cursive alphabet frieze above chalkboard was cut apart and stuck to chalkboard to create new upper-grade look to the word wall.
- Dry erase shower board was cut to size and fastened to front of the science table to make a fun writing surface.
- Low stools were added so kids can sit and use the top of the table as a writing "desk," too.
- Writing tools and a lamp are added to make this an inviting space.

Computer Station BEFORE

- Long tables take up a lot of wall space.
- Clutter on walls can be distracting to some students.
- Not much room for student work to be displayed.

Computer Station AFTER

- Computers were moved to smaller trapezoid tables to take up less wall space.
- New bulletin board color and stuff removed from walls gives this a cleaner, more open look and leaves room for student work.

Back Wall of Classroom BEFORE

- Furniture stored along this back wall was not well utilized—we moved the brown shelves to the new classroom library; green shelves moved to front of whole-group teaching area for storage.
- Trapezoid tables could become clutter magnets, but are converted to new literacy stations . . . buddy reading and listening, as follows.

NEW Buddy Reading Station

- Plastic buckets turned upside down make fun seating (or can be used for storage).
- Dollar store baskets will hold buddy reading materials as these are introduced through shared reading (whole group) or small-group reading instruction.
- A small, fun rug helps define the space.

NEW Listening Station

- Fabric skirt attached with Velcro to table creates additional storage space.
- Baskets and pencil cup are added for response sheets and writing utensils to be used after modeled well in whole-group instruction.
- Clipboards may be used while kids write responses during and/or after listening to a tape.

Old Built-In Cabinet Against Back Wall BEFORE

- This is a clutter magnet/catchall space.
- Cabinet is old and ugly, so we were given permission to refinish it.

Word Study Station AFTER

- We primed the cabinet doors with several coats of magnetic paint.
- When dry, we painted the doors with chalkboard paint—now we have a magnetic chalkboard space where students can build words and write them in chalk at the word study station.
- Containers for storing materials were added on top to make them easily accessible to kids and keep this area neat.

Entry BEFORE

There's a whole lot going on! Visual clutter! Unused furniture is destined to become a clutter magnet.

Imagine the entrance as the filter for the outside world. It should draw you in and make you feel like you want to stay here. It should say, "Welcome."

Entry AFTER

We've chosen blue, a calming color, as the major element that ties the room together and makes it less visually distracting for students. The space is ready for student work. Furniture is used for student learning, rather than to stack stuff.

Q: *"How can I arrange my furniture in a new way? I get tired of it always looking the same."*

A: It's not about YOU. Kids need consistency! They like (and need) order in the classroom. Changing it too often can create confusion.

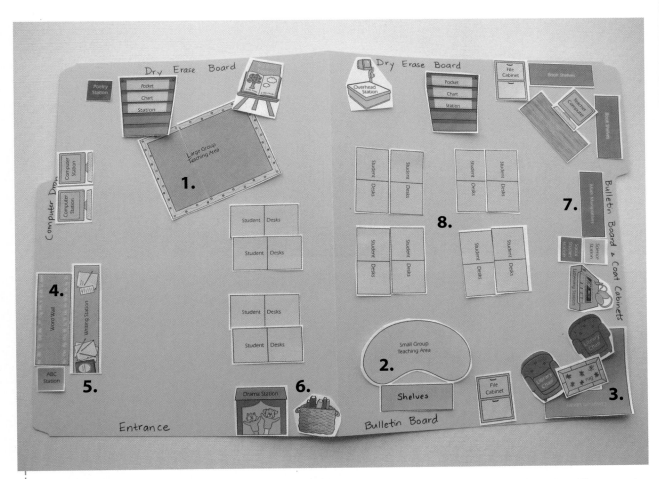

Here's one look at a classroom space. We used a classroom mapping tool from www.reallygoodstuff.com and planned it on paper, then arranged the furniture for maximizing instruction. Numbers show the order in which this room was set up. Permanent fixtures were written on the perimeter of a file folder. Pieces representing classroom spaces and furniture were placed on top and moved around to arrange the room, as explained in Chapter 1, "Planning Your Space."

1. Whole-group teaching area
2. Small-group teaching area
3. Classroom library
4. Word wall
5. Writing station
6. Drama and buddy reading stations
7. Math manipulatives and science/social studies stations
8. Desks (student and teacher)

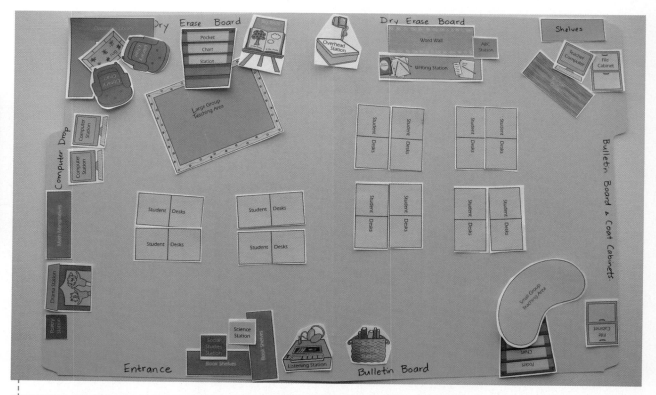

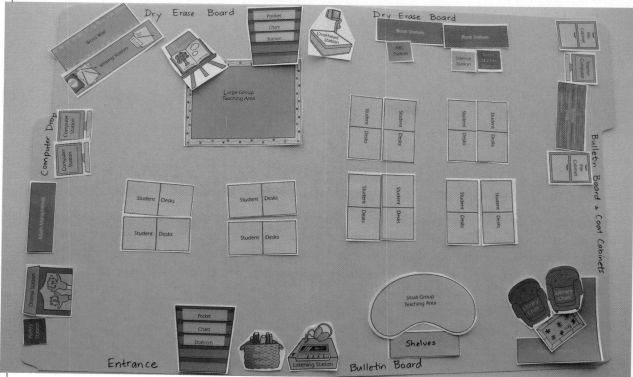

Here are two more possible setups for this same classroom.
- Discuss what you like best about the room designs.
- Think about which arrangement you'd choose and why.

Q: *"How can I make room for another adult in my classroom? A Title I teacher, an inclusion teacher, a paraprofessional?"*

A: Give them a bit of space, but make it double duty, if possible. A resource teacher coming into your room for part of the day may have to teach in small group at a bank of student desks or a table that kids sit at during another time of day. A paraprofessional shouldn't be sitting at a desk all day long, but should be helping you to teach and monitor. Consider a small area for this person to keep her things. You DO NOT need TWO TEACHER DESKS. This takes up too much space in most classrooms.

Title I teacher meets with a small group at a bank of student desks while the classroom teacher meets with another group at a table set up for this purpose.

This small round table is used as space for a teacher assistant to meet with small groups in this portable building. It also works as a word study station when the assistant is not there. This space also doubles as a place for the assistant to store her stuff when not working with a group.

The classroom teacher in the same room has a separate table set up for small group in this portable building. This space does double duty as her desk, too.

Q: Help! I have very few electrical outlets.

A: Be creative. Use tape recorders or CD players that use batteries instead of plugs. Duplicate some of your stations that don't need electricity.

- Use a battery-powered CD player for listening.
- Attach a splitter so two kids can listen with earphones at once.
- Pictures and directions posted right here help kids be independent.

Battery-operated tape recorder, books, and response sheets stored in this portable listening station can be used anywhere in the room.

A Thought on Arranging . . . Think "Double Duty" When Setting Up Your Furniture

Consider two low filing cabinets rather than one tall one. Use as room dividers and magnetic spaces.

- *What do you have that can serve multiple purposes?*
- *If something is only used for 10 minutes a day, it's not worth the space it's occupying in a limited-space classroom.*

File Cabinets Can Serve Multiple Purposes . . .

Storage

Magnetic Space for ABC Station with Fridge Phonics by Leap Frog

Letter Sorting on Magnetic Space

Word Sorting at Word Study Station

A Teacher Desk Can Serve Multiple Purposes . . .

Use the front of your teacher desk to hold small pocket charts easily accessible for children. These can be used for a pocket chart station or a poetry station. Materials to be used here are stored in baskets under the teacher desk to save space.

The front of this teacher desk is used for building singular, plural, proper, and possessive nouns with magnetic letters. Letters are stored under the desk to save space. Weekly Reader is used as source for reading and finding types of nouns at this station.

Backs of Shelves Can Serve Multiple Purposes . . .

Small pocket charts can hang on the back of low shelves to create a room divider and make extra room for a pocket chart station.

Paint the back of low shelves with magnetic paint as primer and then chalkboard paint over top. Now kids can use it to work with magnetic letters and build words. They can also write words with chalk.

A Chalkboard/Dry Erase Board Can Serve Multiple Purposes . . .

Part of this large dry erase board is used for a first-grade word wall in this portable building. The words have little bits of magnetic tape on the back and can be moved on and off the wall by kids.

This chalkboard is *not* magnetic. The teacher attached magnetic strips to the board to make the word wall magnetic and interactive. She will put a piece of magnetic tape on the back of each word as she adds it to the word wall.

A Bulletin Board Can Serve Multiple Purposes . . .

This bulletin board is turned into a backdrop for a housekeeping center in a pre-K or K classroom. Environmental print and/or menus can be added to the bulletin board throughout the year. Ask students to bring in print and menus from home to add to this area.

The bulletin board was moved near the writing station in this portable building to use as a display space for student writing. Have children choose their best work to hang here for their friends to read.

The pocket chart is stapled low onto a bulletin board so kids can use it for a pocket chart or a poetry work station.

Next Steps/Things to Try

1. Arrange your room with a friend. Use your planning map as a guide. Try setting up the desks last, not first. What impact did this have on your final room arrangement?
2. What is your favorite part of your room? Why? What is the part the kids like best? What do they like best about it?
3. What part of your room do you like the least? Why? Take a look at this part of the room with a colleague and discuss how to tweak the space to make it work better. Your students may have good ideas on this, too.
4. What tips from this chapter did you find most helpful? What will you try in your room?
5. What furniture/spaces in your classroom do double duty? What might you be able to use for multiple purposes?
6. Where are you on this continuum for arranging your room? Think about next steps you'd like to take.

```
◄─────────────┬──────────────┬──────────────┬─────────────►
              1              2              3              4
```

1. I didn't arrange my furniture. It was like this when I moved into my room. OR, I've always set up my room like this. I'm kind of used to it. OR, I change my room around constantly. I can't seem to find a way it works for me.
2. There are some parts of my room that aren't working so well. I'll ask my literacy coach or another teacher to help me pinpoint where to start.
3. I'm going to rethink my _____ teaching space. I'll choose several ideas from this book and my conversations with colleagues and kids to help me improve it.
4. I'm going to look critically at how we use space in our classroom. Next time I set it up, I'm using the order described in this book. For now, I'm going to watch to see how my kids are using the space. Then I'll fine-tune spaces using ideas from this chapter.

Chapter 3

Come On In!

Whole-Group Area
Small-Group Area
Classroom Library
Literacy Work Stations
Desks/Tables

picture is worth a thousand words. Teachers often comment that they love all the pictures of classrooms I show at conferences and staff development sessions when teaching about literacy work stations and small-group instruction. These photographs help them visualize what they'd like their classrooms and teaching to look like. This chapter is filled with photos for you to study as you think about your own room and teaching in every classroom space.

You'll notice that it is organized, space by space, according to the order used in Chapter 2, "Arranging Your Room." This is to help you think about the places in your room, one at a time, and demonstrate how each area will link to instruction and help students become independent. What will you need in this space to help students stay engaged? How will you organize your teaching materials so they're easily accessible (for both you and your children)?

Teachers and administrators have asked me, "What do we really *need* in each space?" So, you'll find recommendations for must-haves as well as things you might like someday (when you have a few extra dollars). These charts of things to think about in each space (also found in Chapter 1, "Planning Your Space") are repeated here so you can more easily apply the ideas as you go. Besides, I've learned that if you see or hear something several times, you should pay attention to it; it's really important!

The photos in this chapter come from a wide variety of elementary classrooms in different grade levels across the country, from the mountains of West Virginia to inner-city Houston and the ever-changing suburbs of Indianapolis and Chicago. Most of the pictures are from small-space classrooms and include temporary or portable buildings (affectionately called t-shacks where I live). Some of these rooms may look big, but they're not. In fact, removing clutter from any space will make it appear larger. These photos are not from large classrooms, because they are not the norm.

You'll find ideas for whole-group and small-group teaching areas as well as classroom libraries. If you already teach with literacy work stations, you'll find many examples in this chapter that will give you new ideas of how to keep these fresh and alive in your classroom. If you don't teach with stations, you will still find many useful suggestions you can adapt. The ideas here can be applied to many classrooms across a wide variety of contexts.

Many teachers ask if there are desks in the rooms where I've worked. Of course there are! It's just that the other spaces take precedence in the teaching, so you don't notice the desks as readily. At the end of this chapter is a section on desks and tables for both teachers and students. Included are suggestions for how to keep your desk from becoming a dumping ground (something I personally fight daily).

At home in my living room, I have a large basket filled with magazines I enjoy reading, including *Real Simple, Cottage Living,* and *Better Homes and Gardens*. You'll always find a recent *Pottery Barn* catalog here, as well, for inspiration. I pore through the pages of these texts over and over again, searching for the perfect way to organize my bookshelves or arrange objects on my mantel. Recently, a coffee table book, Bunny Williams's *Point of View*, was added to my collection. These large, colorful photos help me as I reflect on my space. My home, my office, and the classrooms where I work are always evolving as I strive to stay current and comfortable in these places.

Open the pages of this chapter and come with me around the country, to classroom environments that support teachers as they teach and help students learn more independence. As you read, make notes of the ideas you'll try.

Whole-Group Area

What is the purpose of this space? How does it link to instruction? What materials will we need here?

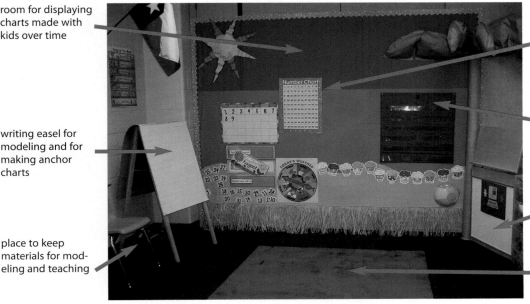

room for displaying charts made with kids over time

calendar and math charts for large-group math time

pocket chart for modeling

writing easel for modeling and for making anchor charts

Big Book easel for shared reading

place to keep materials for modeling and teaching

rug to define the space

MY INSTRUCTION	SPACE I'LL NEED	THOUGHTS ON SETTING UP
more modeling in whole group	whole-group teaching area	• place near the board where I can chart things • large rug to define the space • place to keep books and writing stuff I'm teaching with

ESSENTIALS/MUST-HAVES	OTHER THINGS YOU MIGHT LIKE HERE	LINK TO INSTRUCTION
Whole-Group Area • large rug/carpet squares/mats to define whole-group teaching area • Big Book easel/writing easel • overhead projector or document camera on cart • calendar area for math	**Whole-Group Area** • comfy teacher chair (if you have space) • laundry basket for Big Book storage • small shelves for storing teacher materials needed for the day	**Whole-Group Area** • modeling how to read, write (and learn math, science, and social studies) • read-aloud, shared reading, modeled and shared writing, calendar work, group discussions, sharing time

More Whole-Group Areas

In this fourth-grade classroom, the teacher pulls students up to the whole-group area for read-aloud, shared reading, and modeled writing lessons. Note the anchor charts she has made with the class on the wall. She sits in a rocker and has all materials for the day in the fabric stacking bins beside her chair. Kids sit on and around the rug.

Again, students can gather on this fun rug in another classroom. They will sit on and behind it. This brings them up close to the teacher so they pay better attention. The teacher sits on a stool and uses the Big Book/writing easel for modeling how to read and write. Math charts are on one side of her bulletin board and reading charts on the other.

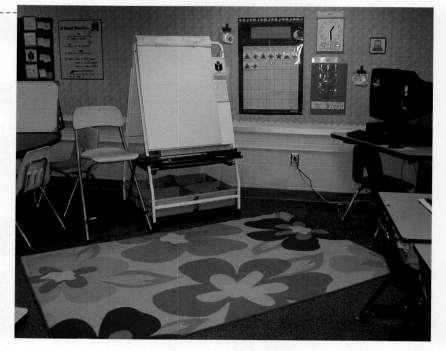

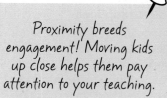

Proximity breeds engagement! Moving kids up close helps them pay attention to your teaching.

Here, a teacher has used space below the boards for displaying charts she is using for teaching. She has also divided her bulletin boards into spaces for both reading and math. There is ample space for kids to gather on the rug, but desks are placed right next to the edge so there is plenty of room for all the furniture, too. In this room, the teacher sits in a chair to be close to their eye level. She'll demonstrate reading and writing using the easel and dry erase board in her whole-group area.

An upper-grade classroom has an inviting whole-group area for teaching. Silk plants, party lights, and comfy seating make this a fun place for learning. It's used for two purposes—a meeting area and the classroom library. Bookshelves were made by placing boards (covered in contact paper) on top of cement blocks. Things are also stored neatly under the shelves. The teacher draws names weekly for who will sit in the special chairs and beanbags during whole group, so everyone has a turn over time.

Note: These classrooms do have a student desk for each child. Desks are placed right next to the edge of spaces pictured here.

Small-Group Area

What is the purpose of this space? How does it link to instruction? What materials will we need here?

anchor charts made with kids in whole group

portable dry erase/magnetic easel for demos

small-group teaching materials at teacher's fingertips

lesson plan notebook and reading groups folder

small-group table for 4–6 kids plus teacher

MY INSTRUCTION	SPACE I'LL NEED	THOUGHTS ON SETTING UP
daily small-group instruction	small-group teaching area	• have a clear view of all stations so I can see what rest of the class is doing • put near a bulletin board so I can display anchor charts • put shelves and baskets there to hold small-group materials • label containers holding materials for easy storage and retrieval

More Small-Group Areas

This small-group area is in the corner of a portable building. It's a small room, but the teacher values small-group instruction and devoted a special space for it. She placed it near a bulletin board to have room to post anchor charts she'll need in small group.

ESSENTIALS/MUST-HAVES	OTHER THINGS YOU MIGHT LIKE HERE	LINK TO INSTRUCTION
Small-Group Area • table for small-group teaching • shelves or clear plastic drawer units for small-group reading materials behind the table • place this by a bulletin board/display space (to post anchor charts)	**Small-Group Area** • 6 dry erase boards and markers • tabletop dry erase/magnetic easel • 6 sets of magnetic letters (lowercase) • plastic tackle box for storing magnetic letters • anchor charts (developed with kids)	**Small-Group Area** • supporting 4–6 kids at a time as readers, writers, thinkers, mathematicians in small-group instruction • small groups for reading, writing, or math; literature discussion group meetings

This colored file organizer keeps all things needed for each day in small group. Each group has a different color.

In both of these classrooms, the teacher has a well-organized small-group area. All materials are right where they're needed for effective instruction. The teacher uses shelves or stacking drawers to house small-group teaching materials. There is a board for teaching nearby as well.

Some itinerant teachers, such as Title I or special education,
"push in" to classrooms during small-group reading time.
Here are some ideas of how they organize their materials:

Materials needed for small group are carried from classroom to classroom in a sturdy plastic tub. The itinerant teacher's schedule is displayed on the front to help her keep on time throughout the day.

TIME	MON. – FRI.
8:00 – 8:30	IPAP/TECH
8:30 – 9:15	FUNK
9:15 – 10:00	HAINES
10:00 – 10:45	HARDINGER
10:45 – 11:30	HOTT/VANMETER

Small-Group Area

Lesson plans are kept on a clipboard stored in the tub.

Phonics charts, word cards, little books for reading, and sticky notes are also kept in the tub.

So are dry erase supplies (enough for 6 kids), question cards, word tiles for making sentences, and mechanical pencils with built-in erasers. All materials needed are at the teacher's fingertips.

Small-group teaching materials stored in three stacking draw-ers help classroom teachers organize their small-group space. At the end of a small-group lesson, students can help put away materials from the session, while the rest of the class cleans up their literacy work stations.

totes filled with sticky notes, pens, and other tools for teacher

dry erase boards stored on bottom due to weight, and dry erase materials stored in drawer above it

books for each reading group in drawer with colored label to match for easy retrieval and storage

other supplies needed in labeled draw-ers—magnetic letters, paper and sen-tence strips, sticky notes, highlighter tape, etc.

Don't put wheels on stacking drawers and they won't break; use the last minute of small-group time to have kids help return materials to appropriate spaces in the small-group area while the rest of the class tidies up literacy work stations

Anchor charts made with students hang in the small-group teaching area to help kids make connections to skills previously taught.

Comprehension Chart

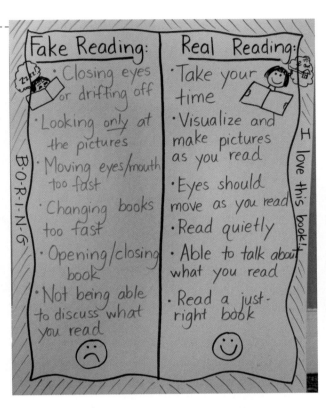

Phonics Charts

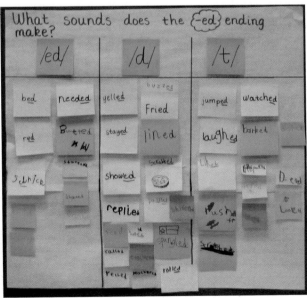

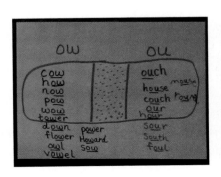

Classroom Library

What is the purpose of this space? How does it link to instruction? What materials will we need here?

bulletin board nearby for displaying book reviews, anchor charts for book selection, etc.

bookshelf angled in the corner to invite children into this space

small rug to define the space

other low bookshelves for easy access to books for kids; clear plastic shoeboxes ready for books to be sorted by kids

comfy child-size seating

To facilitate student ownership in the classroom library:
· Have students help to sort books. This helps them more easily find and return books to the right place.
· They can help to make labels for book baskets, too.
· Children can write book recommendations/reviews to post in the display space here to help each other with book choice.

A third grader signs out a book from the classroom library. Note the baskets with labels to help with book choice.

MY INSTRUCTION	SPACE I'LL NEED	THOUGHTS ON SETTING UP
independent reading with self-selected books	classroom library	• labeled baskets to help students find books that are just right • nonfiction and fiction shelves • room to display anchor charts to aid book choice

ESSENTIALS/MUST-HAVES	OTHER THINGS YOU MIGHT LIKE HERE	LINK TO INSTRUCTION
Classroom Library • bookshelves • plastic shoeboxes or baskets for books • labels for book baskets (made WITH kids)	**Classroom Library** • small rug to define the space • silk plants • comfy kid-size chairs/pillows • lamp • display space for anchor charts on book choice and related reading strategies and book reviews	**Classroom Library** • place to self-select books for independent reading • cozy area to read in during literacy work stations • place to practice what we've been learning about: genre, authors, content, strategies

This upper-grade classroom has a sophisticated look to lure students in to read. The space also doubles as a whole-group teaching area. Note the organization of books in baskets. Labels that name and picture the author (or topic or genre) or his books make these book baskets more appealing. Labels are made from index cards, laminated and hole-punched, then added to the baskets with one-inch metal book rings. NOTE: The baskets are woven plastic with holes in them.

Nonfiction books are in blue baskets on one shelf.

A shower curtain serves as a divider from the hallway in this open classroom.

Built-in partition provides separation from the hallway and makes a display space for anchor charts and a genre wall in an open classroom.

Folding camp chairs are fun and accessible to kids. They pull them right up to the shelves to browse books, and the chairs can be folded up and stored to save space.

Washable dark blue and green pillows are used for comfortable seating here, too.

The Genre Wall is labeled *fiction* and *nonfiction* in white and blue to match the baskets in the library. As the teacher reads aloud a book to introduce a specific genre, a picture of that book cover is added to anchor it in students' memory.

Categories on this display include:

- Fiction: realistic, humorous, historical, traditional, science
- Nonfiction: biography, informational (science and social studies related), auto-biography

Simple labels with pictures help children choose and return classroom library books easily in this pre-K classroom. The books also reflect what the teacher has been teaching about.

Rain gutters fastened to a cement block wall expand space to display books in this classroom library.

A child-size pool makes an inviting reading space in this first-grade classroom library. Several baskets of books are labeled and provided to simplify book choice at the start of the school year.

A beach umbrella and child-size folding chairs anchored by a rug make this library inviting.

This classroom library has a garden theme and is anchored by indoor-outdoor carpeting to resemble grass. A white picket fence attached to the back of plastic shelves (with plastic ties) helps to define the space. Books are also stored in planters with silk plants added for a bit of life.

Instead of placing all books in one classroom library, some teachers have "satellite libraries" throughout the room:

Here, books are placed in various parts of the room. A basket of books about social studies is kept in a social studies work station.

Nursery rhyme books are kept in a basket by the pocket chart station along with poetry and other activities for sorting and sequencing. Sentence strips with nursery rhymes are written on them for kids to practice reading fluently here. NOTE: in this picture, children have been working with compound words, another thing being studied.

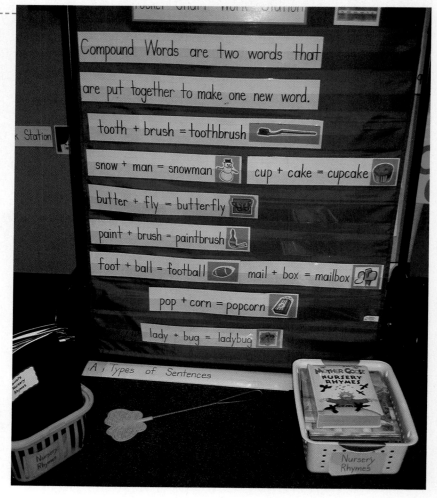

In another classroom, baskets of books are stored on desks or tables around the room. They are organized by topic, genre, or author to make book choice easier for students.

In this second-grade classroom, the teacher has no bookshelves, so she keeps baskets of books in areas on the floor around her room. Note the book reviews written with the class that are posted right above the books on what could have been wasted wall space.

Browsing boxes for pairs of students and a basket of "Our Class Books" are kept on top of shelves for easy student access in this kindergarten room.

Writing Area/Work Station

What is the purpose of this space? How does it link to instruction? What materials will we need here?

An "I Can" list is generated with kids to help them remember what to practice here.

Anchor charts are written with the class to give them writing ideas and vocabulary they might use.

Holiday vocabulary words are provided in books and on cards to use as word banks while writing.

Several kinds of pencils and pens are available. Writers need to choose the materials they'd like to use to communicate their messages at this station.

Sample of how to write each letter of the alphabet is here to help kids with letter formation.

A variety of paper is provided in labeled stacking trays so kids can choose what they'd like to use.

A folding chart houses writing helps to provide support for students to write independently in this small space occupied by two desks covered with a dollar store tablecloth.

MY INSTRUCTION	SPACE I'LL NEED	THOUGHTS ON SETTING UP
writer's workshop	• whole-group teaching area • student desks grouped in 4s and 5s • writing station	• large writing easel at front of room • place to keep writing folders in the file boxes, possibly near the writing station so kids can work with them there for extra practice • status of the class board

ESSENTIALS/MUST-HAVES	OTHER THINGS YOU MIGHT LIKE HERE	LINK TO INSTRUCTION
Writing Area/Work Station • small table or two desks pushed together • trays for stacking and organizing paper • container for writing utensils	**Writing Area/Work Station** • writing supports (dictionaries, thesaurus, writing models) • student mailboxes • fun kid-size chairs • bulletin board nearby	**Writing Area/Work Station** • may be a place for materials to be stored for writer's workshop • space to practice writing during literacy work stations time

A well-organized writing station in a portable classroom maximizes space with a pegboard, bulletin board, baskets, and skirted area for additional storage. Everything kids need is at their fingertips.

Clips from Lakeshore Learning help create a gallery for student writing displayed in this writing station.

Tall stools/chairs make this countertop a handy place for a writing station. Materials needed are stored in a foldable pocket unit from Lakeshore Learning.

A pegboard mounted on the wall in another classroom provides space for writing tools to be stored in the open. Student work can be displayed on the pegboard or on the wall beside it.

Literacy Work Stations

Sight words and writing tips are easily accessed by students at this writing station. Writing utensils, like pencils and crayons, are stored in containers attached to the pegboard, too.

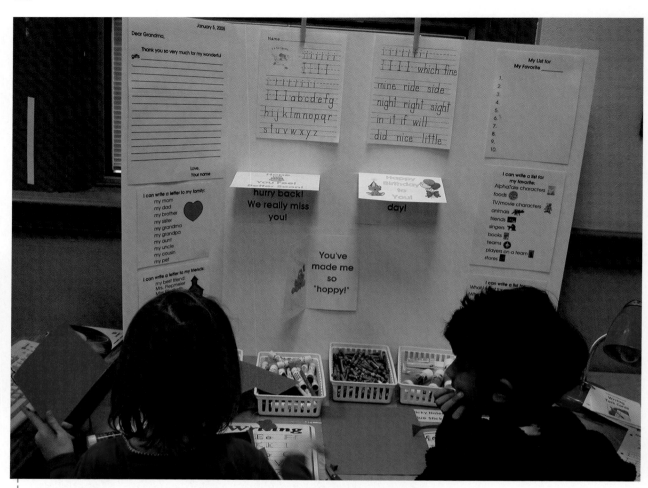

A tri-fold project board provides help and ideas for student writers at this station.

In kindergarten, these writing samples, word banks, and an alphabet chart help support young writers to work independently. Note the fun "pencil" chairs.

Here's another example of writing models from a different classroom. This helps kids know what they can do to practice here.

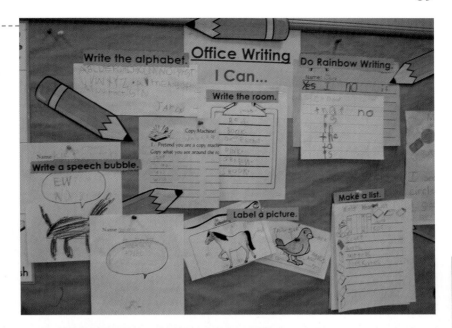

Writing practice is linked to genres and stories being studied in this classroom. Students use vocabulary from this "satellite" word wall made of library pockets to write responses to books read. The "I Can" list is posted on a clipboard here to encourage independence.

Computer Work Station

What is the purpose of this space? How does it link to instruction? What materials will we need here?

"I Can" list generated with the class is posted at the computer station to help kids remember which programs to use.

Three computers provide practice for 3–6 students. If kids share a computer, one uses the keyboard and the other operates the mouse.

ESSENTIALS/MUST-HAVES	OTHER THINGS YOU MIGHT LIKE HERE	LINK TO INSTRUCTION
Other Literacy Stations • computers • ABC/word study • listening • Big Books • baskets or clear plastic containers for portable stations • "I Can" lists or directions written with students • management board	**Other Literacy Stations** • overhead, pocket chart, buddy reading, drama, poetry, etc. • materials to support above stations • tri-fold project boards (for portable stations) • storage unit for portable stations (wire cubes, milk crates, etc.)	**Other Literacy Stations** • places for students to practice reading and writing skills *previously taught* in whole group and/or small group

The computer station is a stationary station. It will have to be placed close to a computer drop. Arrange areas nearby so kids aren't distracted by facing the computer screens. Don't put your small-group area too close by. Headphones are recommended at the computer to minimize noise. Teach kids to remove them if they want to tell their partner something to keep them from shouting at this station.

This space-saving computer table houses three computers and holds the class TV on top (used for viewing morning announcements).

Simple directions (with pictures) for how to use a computer program are posted on the side of a computer to help students work independently here.

Teach children to put a sticky note on the computer telling what's wrong if the computer stops working rather than interrupt the teacher during small group.

ABC/Word Study Work Station

What is the purpose of this space? How does it link to instruction? What materials will we need here?

Sticky notes show vowel patterns being studied. Kids make words from the poem that match, as shown, with magnetic letters on the side of a file cabinet.

Students work with vocabulary here, too, and tally how often they've used the words. Chart is from www.steckvaughn.com.

Photo cards are posted to promote discussion and oral language development and to help kids use their vocabulary words.

Magnetic letters are stored in a labeled fishing tackle box to make it easier for students to find the letters they need for word building.

Students use Wikki Stix to circle words with patterns being studied, as shown above in Big Book.

The "I Can" list helps kids remember the variety of things they can practice at this station.

A magnetic cookie sheet hangs below the magnetic chalkboard "word wall," so kids can build words there. Other word study materials can be stored in portable baskets to the left.

In another classroom, an automotive drip pan mounted to the back of a shelf unit with industrial-strength Velcro makes a space-saving place to work with magnetic letters for making words.

Photos on this "I Can" list help students remember what to do when they come to this station. The class brainstormed the list together; then the teacher typed the list and added digital photos.

A skirted table provides much-needed storage space in most classrooms and provides a surface for word work at this ABC/word study station. Magnetic letters, dry erase materials, and word tiles are stored in containers.

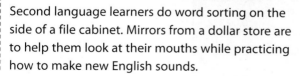

Second language learners do word sorting on the side of a file cabinet. Mirrors from a dollar store are to help them look at their mouths while practicing how to make new English sounds.

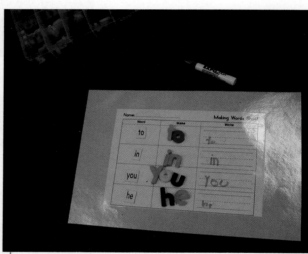

Kids use this portable word study activity on the floor. They build and write words, using magnetic letters.

Listening Work Station

What is the purpose of this space? How does it link to instruction? What materials will we need here?

A sample response is posted to show kids how to respond after listening along with an "I Can" list.

Directions with colored dots (that match those on the recorder) help kids work independently in this kindergarten classroom.

Task cards from www.trcabc.com hang from a ring and give kids ideas of what they can do here.

Headsets hang on chairs or table after kids use them.

Picture directions are in English and Spanish in this bilingual classroom.

Headsets hang from oversized thumbtacks for neat storage.

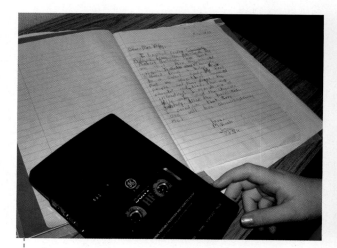

The tape recorder can also be used as a "Recording Studio Work Station," as pictured here. Students read their writing into the tape recorder and then listen back to self-evaluate their reading fluency using a fluency rubric.

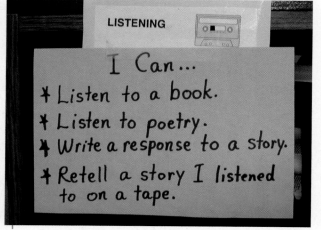

An "I Can" list generated *with* students is posted at the listening station to help them work independently of the teacher.

Big Book Work Station

What is the purpose of this space? How does it link to instruction? What materials will we need here?

"I Can" list written with students reminds them what to do in this second-grade classroom.

Photo of kids working well here shows them what is expected.

Big Books that have been used in whole-group time are used for practice here. Students practice strategies previously modeled, including those relating to phonics, fluency, comprehension, and vocabulary.

Pieces of highlighter tape are stuck onto cards clipped onto the easel. Kids use these to highlight new vocabulary or words with particular phonics patterns being studied.

Bilingual students enjoy reading together and build their fluency at this Big Book station.

Big Books are stored in a tall, wide laundry basket beside the Big Book easel. Pointers and other tools are in a smaller basket clipped onto the laundry one.

At this kindergarten Big Book station, tools for practice with Big Books are stored at the bottom of the easel (which is a dry erase/magnetic space). Kids can use task cards (left), highlighting devices (middle), and the "I Can" list (right) to help them stay on task.

Pocket Chart Work Station

What is the purpose of this space? How does it link to instruction? What materials will we need here?

"I Can" list with photos made *with* students is posted to help students work independently.

Pocket chart is stapled to the bottom half of a bulletin board to save wall space and make this easy for kids to reach.

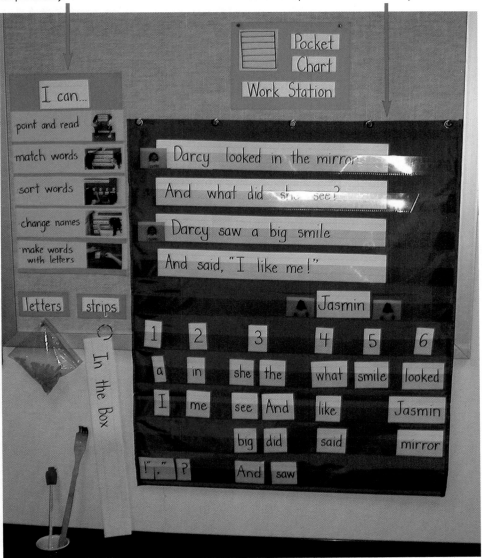

Materials needed here are organized and at kids' fingertips to eliminate interrupting the teacher for help: pointers, plastic letters, sentence strips, word cards, etc.

A desktop pocket chart is portable and saves space. Several pocket charts allow students to do different kinds of activities here, such as reading a poem fluently (on the left) and adding punctuation (made from colored macaroni on cards) on the right.

Pocket chart activities for beginning readers help them learn about print using their names and environmental print—what they know.

Overhead Work Station

What is the purpose of this space? How does it link to instruction? What materials will we need here?

- *Transparencies can be projected on a variety of surfaces: chalkboard (as pictured), dry erase board, wall, easel, etc.*
- *No extra space is needed. Kids practice with what you've already taught.*

A transparency used during whole-group instruction is now used independently by students at the overhead station. They project it onto a chalkboard and write their answers with chalk. The teacher can easily check their work by looking up from his small-group teaching area.

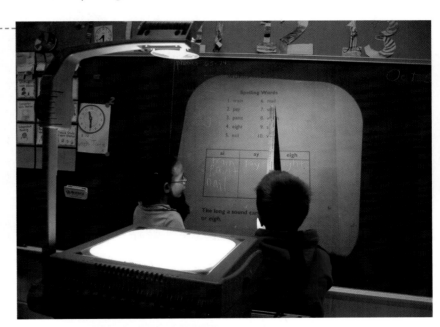

Here, two students project a poem from the overhead onto a low dry erase easel. They read and reread the poem (taught with in class) for fluency and expression. Then they look for words representing phonics patterns being taught.

Literacy Work Stations

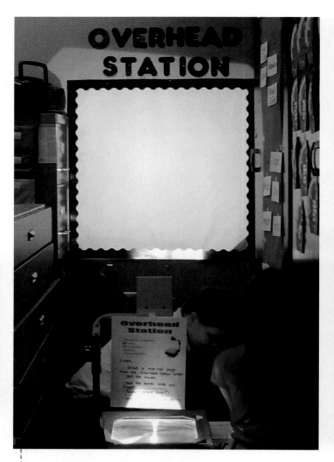

An overhead can project onto a wall space in an unused corner of the classroom.

This low overhead cart on wheels was made by a parent volunteer.

Recycling Tip: Use trimmed pieces of leftover laminating film, and have kids place these on top of any fill-in-the-blank transparency they're working with. They can write on the laminating film with a vis-à-vis marker and take it home to show what they did at school. They could also write a story or nonfiction piece of writing on the laminating film (while a friend helps to edit it on the projected screen) and take this home.

An overhead on a low cart or plant stand can project onto a tri-fold project board.

Portable Work Stations

What might work well as a portable station? Where will I store these neatly? What materials will we need here? Where will students use these in the classroom . . . on the floor, at a desk, in the hall?

Wire cubes on a tabletop create a storage area for portable stations in this fifth-grade room.

Each basket holds a separate station complete with a label naming it and materials needed inside the basket.

Stations include:
- buddy reading
- what would the character do?
- word study
- generalization
- guess my word

Students practice buddy reading using these portable materials stored in a basket. They wear buddy reading visors from a dollar store for novelty (and to keep buddy reading fun).

Upper-grade buddy reading materials are stored in a portable basket and carried to another area of the room where a pair of students works together. Directions were written by the class and are kept in the basket to promote student independence.

Stacking baskets hold ABC/word study materials that can be taken to the floor to use at this station. Materials here include sight words, games, and word sorts in Ziploc bags.

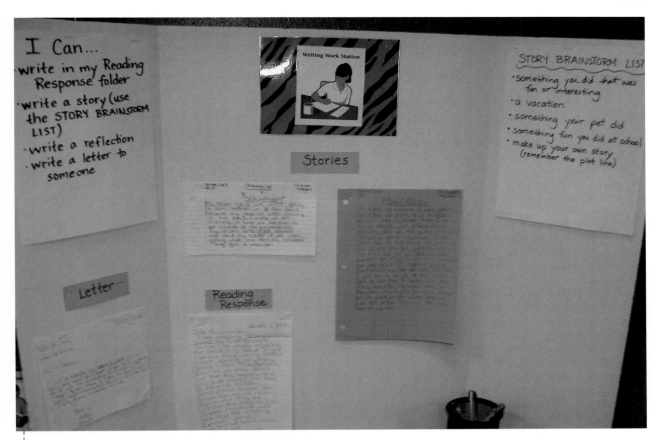

Tri-fold project board is used as a portable writing station. Kids set it on the floor and write on clipboards in this fifth-grade classroom as an extension to the writing they do during writer's workshop. The board holds ideas and student writing samples to give kids ideas for their writing practice here.

A portable drama station for kindergarten includes a retelling board (in background) and props and books for retelling. Task cards for drama from www.trcabc.com are also kept in the basket to help students think about what they can do at this station.

Another portable drama station is pictured here. This one sits atop a desk or can be placed on the floor. Students use scripts or books to act out familiar stories in this first-grade classroom.

Portable poetry stations are used in these two classrooms. In the top photo, poetry books are stored in a basket with poetry task cards from *Practice with Purpose*, p. 203 (Stenhouse, 2005). In the bottom photo, precut and pre-typed poems taught with in shared reading are stored in a basket and can be glued into kids' poetry notebooks where they visualize and illustrate them.

Student Desks/Tables

How will we set up individual places for students? Will they have desks or tables? How will these be arranged to minimize classroom space? How will children use/share supplies? When will students work at their desks/tables?

- Students in kindergarten sit at tables upon arrival in the morning and browse books and/or watch morning announcements on TV.
- Trapezoid tables are used and comfortably seat 6 children at each table.
- Books for browsing are in colored tubs on each table. Name tags identify each child's special place to sit.

ESSENTIALS/MUST-HAVES	OTHER THINGS YOU MIGHT LIKE HERE	LINK TO INSTRUCTION
Desks/Tables • student desks grouped together to save space (groups of 4–6) • teacher desk in small, out-of-the-way space (to maximize room for kids' learning)	**Desks/Tables** • might get rid of teacher desk and use small-group teaching table as desk, too (or use desk for double duty) • use small computer table as teacher desk	**Desks/Tables** • places for students to work independently to practice reading, writing, math, science, social studies, etc. • personal spaces for kids and for teacher

Desks are grouped in sets of 4, 5, or 6 in these classrooms to create work spaces for students. Children keep their supplies and textbooks inside their desks.

Set up desk/table spaces so students have all they need at their fingertips when working here. This will help them work independently, rather than be distracted by going across the room to get supplies.

Pictured is a kindergarten table setup at the start of the year. Journals are in the center, and a caddy holds pencils, markers, glue, and scissors. Each section of the container is marked with a picture and word to help children keep table supplies organized.

In a different kindergarten classroom a bit later in the year, each child has a pencil box with her supplies in it. A tub in the center of the table holds little books for browsing time, a date stamp and stamp pad in a Ziploc bag (for writing workshop time), and an ABC chart to help kids in both reading and writing.

Teacher Desk/Work Space

How much space will I use for my work area? Will I use a traditional teacher desk or use my small-group area? Do I have access to my computer and file cabinet? Where will I keep my things so I can easily find them? How can I provide a model for my students?

Stacking plastic drawers and wooden shelves hold teacher supplies so they are easily accessible.

Small computer work station for the teacher saves space and brings the teacher desk into the twenty-first century.

Small baskets hold smaller supplies to keep these well organized. Labels will help you return things to their proper place.

Desks/Tables

An organized desk greets this teacher as she starts her day with a sense of calm. She keeps ONLY essential items on top of her desk along with a large calendar to jot down important notes. A bulletin board behind the space provides room for important notes to be posted.

This is the inside of two drawers from the desk above. Note the use of small containers to organize her stuff.

We saw Pam's teacher space on the first pages of this book. This is a close-up of containers *with labels* that help her return oft-lost things like scissors to their homes.

Teacher Desk/Small-Group Area BEFORE

This teacher was wasting a lot of precious time because she couldn't easily find what she needed (before, during, and after school). It was impossible to work with a small group here.

Teacher Desk/Small-Group Area AFTER

Everything was removed from the shelves and table and was sorted into piles on the floor . . . keep and give away. The other pile went into the trash can (things you don't need or want). Much of the paper shown in the before photo was not needed, along with dried-up markers and pens, and was recycled or thrown away. Baskets were added and labeled and contain oft-used materials. ABC drawers and a magnetic teaching easel were found on the floor during this makeover!

Teacher Desk Drawer BEFORE

It was hard for this teacher to keep everything neat and organized in her desk drawer. Stuff started to creep out onto the top of her counter.

Teacher Desk Drawer AFTER

The use of small containers (all found in various parts of this classroom) helped create spaces for everything the teacher used on a daily basis. It gave her a sense of calm to open this drawer and easily find what she needed during a hectic day.

My Own Desk/Table

This is the top of my desk. (Actually, it's a writing table.) I keep pens, pencils, and paper clips in antique jars. Important files that I use daily are stored vertically on top of my desk to the left. My At-a-Glance planner is stored in front of the files. Another set of stacking trays (on the right side of my desk) holds important papers related to projects I'm working on. My laptop uses up little space. And I keep my desk memorabilia to a minimum (just one lovely candle, some flowers, and a few photos).

Right behind my desk I have a counter with a built-in drawer. My office chair swivels easily between the two spaces. This drawer is divided into smaller spaces with Rubbermaid drawer organizers that clip together. I was able to create my own drawer organizing system with it. It's a huge time- and space-saver!

Above the counter are shelves where I store all my professional books in clear plastic shoeboxes. Every basket is labeled, so I can easily find what I'm needing while working on my research or training.

------------ HOW DO I KEEP MY DESK FROM BECOMING CLUTTERED? ------------

TEACHER DESK PROBLEM	POSSIBLE SOLUTION
My desk is a mess. Where do I begin?	Start with your desk drawers. Take everything out of them (one drawer at a time), and sort what you find into piles. Throw away unneeded junk, broken pencils, etc. Then label each pile and create a home for it. Use drawer dividers or small containers to create a space for each kind of item as you return it to the drawers.
How can I organize my drawers?	Put things you use often in the front of your drawers and things you don't use regularly toward the back. I like white storage containers since they brighten up my drawers. I put things I use constantly on top of my desk in neat containers.
What do I do with all the little stuff kids give me (or I collect) throughout the day?	Smile and thank your students. Then put the items (leaves, dandelions, etc.) in a little basket labeled "Kid Stuff." Clean it out at the end of each day. If you must confiscate toys students bring to class, you might also place those there. Empty this basket regularly (weekly or monthly). Don't toss these items in your desk.
What should I keep on top of my desk?	Place only things you need *every day* here. You might want to keep a large calendar (or a planner) on your desk or on a nearby wall space. I like to keep files I use daily in a vertical file on top of my desk. I also keep my pens and paper clips here, so I can easily grab them. Keep desk memorabilia (and shrines to your alma mater) to a minimum. Edit your desktop regularly.
I can never find my stapler. Help!	Keep office supplies used daily (pens, scissors, ruler, paper clips, stapler, etc.) in the same place *every day*, and get into the habit of returning them immediately after you use them. Add labels if it will help you put things back. And throw away dried-up markers and pens immediately!
Where do I put all the paper that comes across my desk?	Apply the "junk mail rule" to all paper. Touch it just once. Decide immediately where it goes. Keep one trash can by your desk and another centrally located for kids to use. You might want to keep three drawers or containers nearby labeled "To Do," "To File," and "Still Thinking" to put things in that you can't deal with right away. Then file papers regularly each week, perhaps on Friday afternoons. Work on your "To Do" projects as you have time. Put papers that must be sent home in a crate or basket (labeled "Things to Send Home") by the door to remind you to send them out the door at the end of the day.
What do I do with the materials I need to teach with this week? I tend to stack them on my desk.	You might store these in a filing cabinet or plastic stacking drawers and add labels for each day of the week. Place the materials for each day behind its label or in its own drawer. Reorganize daily or at the end of the week. You could have a label for "Next Week" and put things there you haven't had time to get to.
How can I keep my desk organized?	Have a place for everything and keep everything in its place (both on top of your desk *and* inside your drawers). You *must* set up a system for this, or it will not happen! Keep trying until you find what works for you. Take 5 to 10 minutes *every day* before you leave, and straighten up your desk. When you enter in the morning, your clean desk will energize you and help you face the new day with a smile.

Come On In!

Next Steps/Things to Try

1. Sit in a comfortable place in your classroom and take some time for self-reflection. Use the following questions to think about the overall flow of your classroom:
   a. Which spaces are already well organized?
   b. What makes these areas work well?
2. Look at each space in your classroom and ask these questions: (Work with a friend if you'd like)
   a. What is the purpose of this space?
   b. How does it link to instruction?
   c. Do we have everything we need at our fingertips?
   d. How could we make it work even better?
   Use the spaces in this chapter to give you a way to systematically look at your room and its organization. Start with the whole-group teaching area. Then move to your small-group area, etc.
3. Choose one space in your room that you'd like to better utilize. Work with a colleague to adapt ideas from this chapter to give this area a "fresh start." Take before-and-after pictures and share with your team. Use the forms in the "Resources" section in the back of the book. NOTE: If you have many areas that need work, start with just *one*. Don't overwhelm yourself. Choose one space and get it working well. This will often give you the momentum you need to move to another the next day or the following week.
4. Which ideas from this chapter did you like best? Why? Try several tips and share results with a teammate.
5. Brainstorm ideas from this chapter that will help kids work more independently and will reduce interruptions to the teacher. Try one or two of them and share with your colleagues how these helped classroom management.
6. Where are you on this continuum for thinking about the various areas in your room? Think about next steps you'd like to take.

| 1 | 2 | 3 | 4 |

1. I never thought about my room, area by area, like in this chapter. It was just my classroom.
2. I'll pick one area and start there. I'll read the section on that space and then work on setting it up to work more effectively.
3. I've tried to set up different areas in my classroom. Now I'll fine-tune one or two of them. I will get a colleague to help me think through my space.
4. I'm going to look at each area in this chapter, systematically, and think about my space. I'll start with what's working well and try to identify what's making it work. Then I'll move onto other areas and work with them, one at a time.

his past year, I had an opportunity to study with Heather, a reflective young woman who teaches kindergarten. One thing that struck me about her classroom was that she didn't plaster her walls with a bunch of stuff at the start of the year. I'd found a scholastic soulmate! Each time I'd visit her room, we'd look at her walls together. They told the story of what she valued and what she'd been teaching. Here's a snippet from one of our conversations:

Heather: What do you think about my walls? I've been really thinking about what I'm putting on them this year.

Debbie: They show me exactly what you've been teaching. I can tell that your class has been learning about nocturnal animals in science by the pictures and charts on your science wall. From the charts on another wall, I can see that your students are learning to make all kinds of books as writers. And your word wall has expanded since last time I was here.

117

Heather: My word wall has been working really well. In fact, the kids this year are using it more than any other class I've ever taught. I think it's because they can take the words on and off the wall. Adding magnetic tape to the back of the words and to the wall has made all the difference.

Debbie: Yes, making your word wall interactive is key. And it's placed low so kids can reach it. You are always teaching with your word wall in whole group, too, and modeling helps kids know how to use it. I've noticed that your class is reading and writing many of the words on the wall.

Heather: I've been thinking about moving my ABC chart to my small-group teaching area. Most of my kids know their letters now, and there are just a few who still need help. If I have it close by in small group, I can help them make connections.

Debbie: I agree. And you might also add the ABC chart to their tables, so they can use it during writing time.

While visiting classrooms around the country, I've been surprised by the lack of attention walls often receive. In many cases, it seems that the walls are often the last things that we look at when organizing our classrooms. Thus, this entire chapter is devoted to walls and how to display things to get the most from your teaching. I've found that often we use our dry erase or chalkboards to chart things, but then erase them at the end of the day. For many kids, this information just goes into short-term memory. By creating, displaying, and referring to anchor charts across all subject areas, I believe we can help kids transfer ideas and "anchor" them into long-term memory.

In some rooms, we make so many charts that these just get stuck one on top of another to create what I call the "layered wall." It's hard to tell just what is valued in these rooms. Still other classrooms have bulletin boards covered with so many colors and patterns and multicolored decorative borders that it's hard to pay attention to what is being displayed.

This chapter is filled with photos of thoughtful, well-designed walls and charts. There's a section on word walls due to the number of questions I get about how these should look across grade levels. You might want to take photos of your walls and step back to see the message they are conveying. The biggest advice on walls I can give is to keep them simple. Choose 2 or 3 colors, consider framing your charts with simple borders, and think about what your walls tell your students, your parents, and all visitors to your classroom.

- *I have lots of stuff to hang. Where do I put it all?*
- *How much should I put up before the students start school?*
- *What should really be posted on my walls? My district expects a word wall, calendar math, rules, reading strategy posters, student work, procedural information, etc., and I'm running out of room. Help!*

What you hang on your walls (or cabinets or doors) shows what you value.

In the fall, wall displays are minimal in this classroom to leave space for the children. Blue and green are the predominant colors and create a soothing, welcoming effect.

The books and materials you display in your classroom also show what's important to you. This teacher creates a space for her fifth graders to display self-selected books to encourage classmates to recommend books to each other. These books are displayed prominently in her classroom library on top of a shelf. A label explains the purpose for this display. Anchor charts surround the display for support.

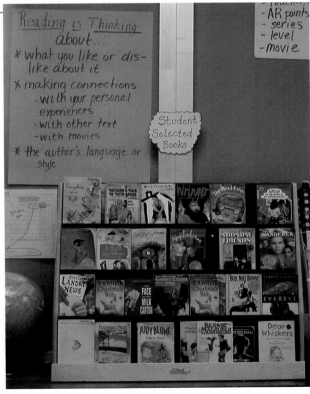

Using Your Walls

Your Walls Tell a Story

Designing Your Wall Space

Step One:

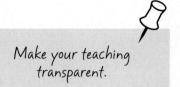

Make your teaching transparent.

THINK about the messages you want your walls to convey. Plan for wall spaces that support the teaching you will be doing.

- Where will instruction take place in my classroom and will I have display space located there to aid and support my teaching (and children's learning) in both whole and small group?
- What are the most important things to display? Where will I place them? (walls, bulletin boards, whiteboards, cabinet doors, hallways)
- How much space will be needed for each display?

MY INSTRUCTION	WHAT I'LL DISPLAY	SPACES I'LL NEED/ CONSIDERATIONS
more modeling in whole-group reading	• anchor charts I make with the class to help them remember what I've been teaching • word wall with high-frequency (K–1) or interesting words (2 and up) or content-area words	• nearby wall to display recent charts I've made with kids (where kids can read these and I can point to them to make reference) • word wall kids can easily see and we can easily add to (near my whole-group area)
daily small-group reading instruction	• anchor charts I've taught with in whole group that I now want to move to small group for reinforcement with kids who need extra support • charts (small versions that match what I've used in whole group) for phonics, comprehension, fluency, writing, and vocabulary	• bulletin board or wall/cabinet display space by small-group area for posting charts • dry erase space may be helpful (or use a tabletop teaching dry erase-magnetic easel)
daily independent reading time	• charts made with kids about how to choose books • displays of recommended books (in classroom library)	• display space in or around the classroom library to post charts
writer's workshop	• anchor charts on how to choose a topic, how to edit, etc. • writing models (by students and teacher)	• large writing easel at front of room • writing gallery (for displaying student writing) • status of the class board

This anchor chart made with first graders helps them remember that stories have a beginning, middle, and end.

THINGS MY SCHOOL/DISTRICT REQUIRES ME TO DISPLAY	WHY IT'S VALUED	WHERE I'LL DISPLAY THIS
• fire exit procedures • class rules	• safety • safety and management	• by the classroom entrance/exit • where kids can see this upon entering to remind them of our agreement of how we'll behave in our classroom
• reading strategy posters	• common language in our school • remind kids to think	• in our whole-group teaching area (as I teach with each one I'll add it) and then move it to small group, as needed
• word wall (high-frequency words in K–2 and interesting vocabulary words in grades 3–6) • content-area word walls or charts	• K–1 kids are learning about print and how words work • grades 2–6 kids need to learn many more content and higher-level vocabulary words	• in pre-K–first grade, find a low space that kids can reach that's by our whole-group teaching area (so I can make links to it while teaching) • in grades 2–6, use a bulletin board or part of a wall to display new vocabulary • create charts of content-area words that change with each new unit of study and hang these in a designated area where kids can easily see and use them
• calendar math display	• daily math teaching is important • routines with visuals will help learning stick	• in whole-group teaching area (different wall space from that used for teaching reading and writing, but can be side by side)

This display has Velcro pieces that show students the supplies they will need to get ready each morning. When students enter the classroom, they read the chart and gather their supplies for the day.

Class rules are brainstormed with the students and remain posted all year long. Kids' self-portraits and signatures personalize this display. An additional chart made with the class reminds them how to handle problems and conflicts in the classroom.

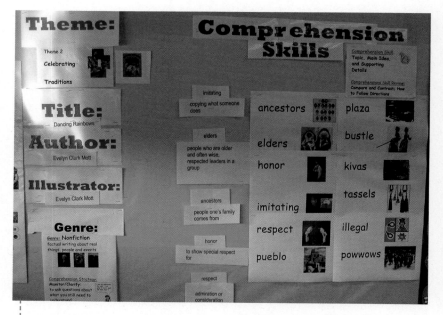

This school requires each teacher to display what he or she is teaching in reading on a "focus wall." It includes objectives and key vocabulary being taught. Note the use of photos to help students learn vocabulary in this third-grade classroom.

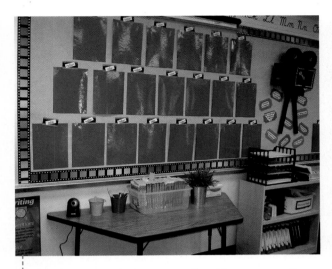

This fourth-grade "writing gallery" has a space for each child to self-select and display a piece of writing for others to read. Blue construction paper sheets with name labels above each provide a space for each student.

Dedicate one set of cabinet doors for places to display student work. Note the variety of work posted here.

Using Your Walls

OTHER THINGS I WILL DISPLAY	WHY IT'S VALUED	WHERE I'LL DISPLAY THIS
student work	• this is the children's classroom and I want to highlight what they're doing	• gallery of work we've done in the classroom (where kids can see and read it) • also use the hallway walls for this so other classes, visitors, and parents can see it
alphabet	• model for ABC order and letter formation	• on student desks and at the writing station so it's at kids' fingertips and they can easily see it (rather than just hanging it up high)
anchor charts made with the class that help them remember the most important things we're learning	• I want kids to use and apply these in their practice	• in our whole-group teaching area (as I teach with each one I'll add it) and then move it to small group, as needed
social studies and science-related pictures/photos, displays	• kids are interested in the world around them • as kids move through the grade levels, they will be required to do more and more nonfiction reading and need this background knowledge	• bulletin board(s) spotlighting science and social studies topics of study

Math anchor charts are displayed on one wall area. Students have been learning about graphing and adding. Note the use of student language and examples on the charts.

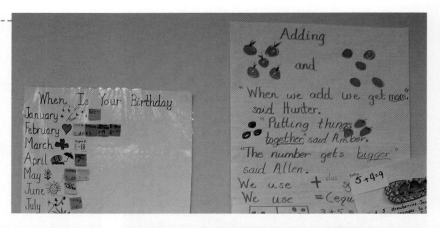

Display of sticky notes generated by students about electricity includes *new things I've learned, connections,* and *questions.* Books and artifacts related to recent units of study on the life cycle and food chain are also posted on this science wall.

| **Step Two:** | Plan which spaces you'll use for what purposes. |

- Start with bare walls.
- You might number your walls and display areas.
- Plan for how much space you'll need for each area. Remember that what you value most may take up more space.
- Look for wall space in unexpected places.
  - Use cabinet doors.
  - Use windows.
  - Don't "decorate" bulletin boards. Use them as instructional spaces.
  - If allowed, hang a clothesline and use it for extra display space.
  - Use hallway space outside your classroom.
  - Create a portable wall space with a tri-fold project board like those used for science fair.
  - Look at how much oversized furniture is in your room. Is it taking up too much wall space? Ask about getting a less obtrusive piece of furniture in its place. (It never hurts to ask!)

THINGS I'LL EDIT/REVISE/NOT PUT ON DISPLAY THIS YEAR	WHY I'M DOING AWAY WITH THESE ITEMS
old alphabet train (that I've been hanging onto for the past 10 years)	• it's faded and I have better things to display that will support instruction
cute cutouts from the teacher supply store (or that I've colored, laminated, and cut out over the years)	• these aren't adding to my instruction—I thought they looked cute when I bought them (or they took a long time to make) • they're adding to the visual clutter in my room • I'd rather have student work or anchor charts displayed
posters I bought from a catalog about punctuation my first year of teaching	• print on them is too small for kids to see from far away • I don't really use them to teach with • they just become wallpaper
word wall that's way up high (near the ceiling)	• my kids can't see the words easily and I can't easily add to the word wall—I'm moving it to a more reachable spot for students
commercial stuff hanging from the ceiling (smiley faces, work zone sign, etc.)	• these are visually distracting for some kids, especially students with behavior disorders and attention problems

These are the walls in one kindergarten classroom in the fall.
Note the use of wall space. What does this teacher value?

When you walk in the room, this wall is to the left.

This is the front wall in this classroom.

This wall is to the right and is being used for storage. NOTE: See Chapter 5, "Organizing Your Stuff," for a makeover of this space!

This wall is in the back of the room.

Step Three: Plan your display spaces.

- Choose 2 or 3 colors only and stick with your plan.
- Cover all bulletin board spaces with the same color paper or fabric to unify your space and create a sense of calm and order in your classroom. USE SOLID COLORS, not prints!
- Use one color of border to frame each display space. Don't use lots of cutesy different borders all over your room. It adds to visual clutter.
- Consider using black as a background for your displays. Print pops out when charts are displayed on top.
- Allow enough space for what you will display at a time. This will avoid the "layered look" of many displays in elementary classrooms.

Too many charts layered over a board are cluttered and hard for students to read or reference.

All bulletin boards are covered with brown paper and framed with animal-print borders to bring consistency and order to the walls in this fifth-grade room. Space to display student writing is neatly organized.

Step Four: Gradually create your displays *as you teach with the materials.*

- Build your classroom wall displays with your children.
- Create charts with students using their words and ideas and illustrations, as appropriate.
- Teach with and refer to these displays in your instruction.
- At the start of the year, reserve some space for student work. Post "coming soon" and "under construction" signs in these spaces.

This hallway display reserves a space for each child's work before school begins. The labels tell parents that student work will be posted here soon.

The teacher places the icons on this pocket chart management board so kids know which literacy work station to go to daily. It is posted on the wall where kids can easily see it, so they can more independently manage where they will work. This is early in the year when kids go to just one station a day.

Several weeks later, kids go to two stations a day. The teacher also will meet with two small groups and uses cards that say "Meet with Me" on the chart. The teacher models and teaches students how to read the board on their own, so she is not interrupted during small group. Thus, her display helps her to teach.

| **Step Five:** | Change your displays as the year goes by. |

- Take things down as students no longer need them. For example, if students have internalized how to sequence, you might remove the anchor chart you've created with them on sequencing. If just a few kids still need it, you might take a digital photo of the chart and move it to your small-group area for reference for those students.

- Replace student work displays every few weeks. Put kids in charge of deciding what they want others to view. By having a student "gallery," this becomes simple. Kids hang up their own work. (Be sure this space is accessible to your students, so they don't have to climb on chairs to post their work.)

- Remove seasonal items when the season has ended. And limit the wall space dedicated to the season. Don't "decorate" your whole room seasonally. It takes up too much valuable teaching space and planning time.

- If you put up things at the start of the year so your walls wouldn't look bare, remove those items after the first few weeks of school. Only display things that you and the students find useful in helping them learn.

- Ask students what they use on the wall. You might take them outside the room and ask them to list everything they use on the walls. Take a look at this survey to make determinations about what's most important to display.

Thoughts on Displaying:

- Are things at students' eye level?
- Is your word wall near the whole-group teaching area?
- Is your calendar in the whole-group teaching area?
- How much space is this display utilizing?
- What kind of background is used for this display? Does it make the display "pop" or does it compete with the materials on display?
- How can you revise to make your displays more user-friendly for kids?

Classroom spaces change throughout the school year. Here are four views of one classroom library over a period of several months.

A pocket chart says, "Chicka, chicka, boom boom, Who will be in our room?"

In late August, the walls are almost bare. Back-to-school books are displayed. Empty baskets are ready for new books.

Several weeks later, children's photos and names are placed in the pocket chart for them to read.

Books about fall take the place of the back-to-school books in the display rack.

A graphic organizer showing story elements is displayed in the library after being used to chart this info in a read-aloud session.

A wall story titled "Our Shape Hunt Book" is written by the class and illustrated in digital photos. It is posted on the wall for children to read.

The book display changes again as new books are read aloud. New baskets in the classroom library reflect author studies of Eric Carle and Kevin Henkes, as well as stories about Corduroy.

In late December, the library is reconfigured to allow space for more books and display of charts and graphic organizers taught with during whole-group instruction.

Displays for young children need to be at their eye level. Use low charts if you run out of wall space.

In this classroom, some "dead space" below the counter was used to display a word wall. An added bonus is that it's at students' eye level.

Likewise, an alphabet frieze is posted under a bulletin board in the whole-group teaching area, which enables the pre-K students in this classroom to easily access it.

Q: As I change my displays, what do I do with all those charts?

A: You might send them home with kids. This extends the learning and strengthens the home–school connection. Before you get rid of the chart, take a digital photo of it and make an 8 ½-by-11-inch colored copy of it. Keep these photos in clear plastic sleeves in a notebook to use in your small-group teaching area or for next year's ideas. Organize them by topic, such as *phonics*, *comprehension*, or *fluency* charts.

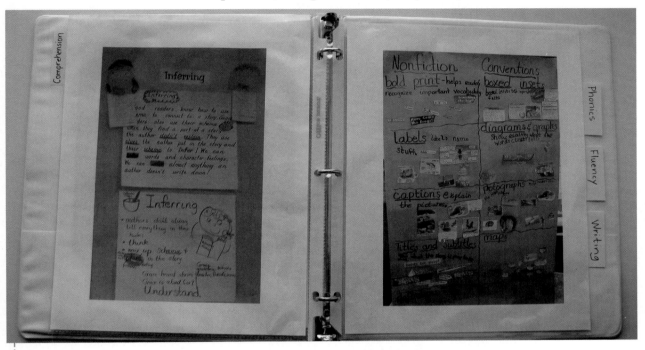

Anchor charts are photographed and stored in a notebook for reference for later in the year or the following school year.

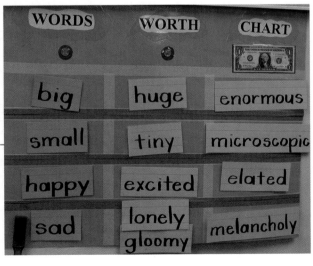

This anchor chart from an upper-grade classroom helps students remember to use more "worthy" words. The teacher challenges kids to use "dollar" words rather than "penny" or "quarter" vocabulary. Words on the chart change periodically as students give examples to show their growing vocabulary.

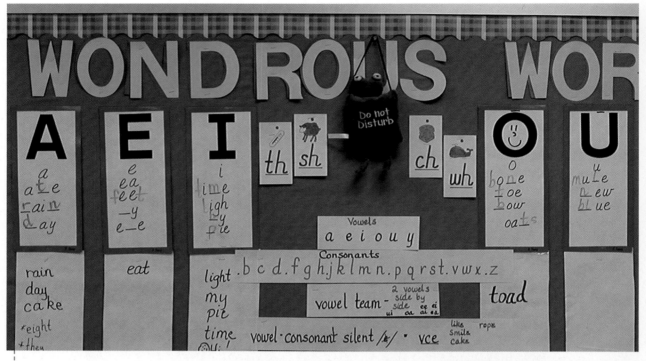

This anchor chart is posted in the small-group area. You can tell that this first-grade teacher has been teaching phonics, focusing on long vowel sounds.

Anchor Chart Tips:
* Use **color** to make anchor charts interesting to look at.
* Consider placing a **border** around each anchor chart. The brain likes borders, because they help to focus and contain the information.
* Use **pictures** (drawings or photos) on each anchor chart. The brain remembers pictures more than words.
* Give each chart a **title**. This helps students focus on the big idea.
* Only make anchor charts for things kids might have trouble **remembering**.

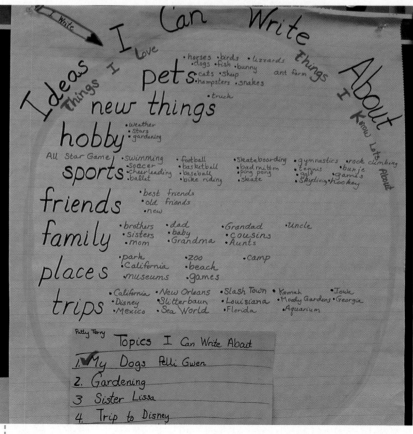

Writing ideas are brainstormed with the class and displayed on this anchor chart by the writing station.

Kindergarten anchor charts displayed on a chalkboard include a names chart, an ABC chart, and a "We Are All Writers" chart to help young children as they learn to read and write.

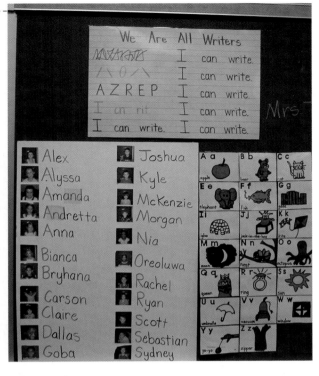

As this class studies nonfiction, they learn about features of text and highlight examples beside this anchor chart. They also jot down samples on sticky notes on the chart.

Q: *What is the best way to display student work?*

A: Use a student work "gallery" where each child chooses his or her best work to display. This could be inside your classroom or in the hallway, depending on your available wall space. Or create murals with your students representing what you've studied.

Each student has a clip with his or her name on it to use for displaying a favorite piece of work on this bulletin board. Note the use of blue and green to keep the display looking "clean."

Fifth graders create a mural about what they learned while studying the water cycle. They add labels, captions, and graphics to the display and use the science book for review.

Q: How can I use my displays to communicate to parents (and other teachers)?

A: Use murals, galleries, and bulletin board displays made with children and post them in the hallways. Include labels describing the work. You might even include information sheets for parents to take home and extend the work you've done at school.

This hallway display shows parents what students are learning about reading in their first-grade classroom. Fluency is a bridge between decoding and comprehension. Students have made cutouts of kids and described each element of reading in their own words. Note the accordion file folder in the bottom left-hand corner, which includes take-home sheets describing ways they can support this learning at home.

A second-grade teacher creates a display to show her colleagues what students have been doing as readers before, during, and after reading. They are focusing on asking good questions to increase their reading comprehension.

This close-up of the above chart shows sticky notes recording kids' questions before reading the book. Book illustrations are used to make the display more visually appealing.

This wall display hangs outside the classroom to tell parents about a visit from the firefighters. It includes photos of children and their classmates.

Q: Where do I put my interactive whiteboard?

A: Find a permanent spot in your whole-group teaching area, if possible, and mount it on the wall to take up less space. These technology tools are wonderful but can take up lots of space.

Q: Do I need to have a "theme" in my classroom for my displays?

A: No, you don't need to center your room around Clifford or bumblebees or even your alma mater! If you must choose a theme, choose "what we're learning."

This display shows what students are learning about in science and math. It is easy to see what is being taught in this classroom. The message is "learning" as the class theme.

Q: How do I know if I have too much on my walls?

A: Take digital photos of your wall displays and examine them. You might be surprised at what you see! Or ask a colleague to look thoughtfully at your displays and give you feedback. Can he or she easily tell what's being taught?

Here are a few suggestions made to the teacher of this primary classroom about her front teaching wall:

- remove some of the busyness, such as all the cutouts of kids
- don't need this many alphabets in one area; take some down and keep one that's easiest for kids to read and use
- ditto for the numbers

Using Your Walls

Q: *I have two classes a day in my room. How do I make/display charts with them?*

A: You might use two different colors of paper (or ink) to create charts for each class. OR make a chart with one class and then ask the other class to add to it.

In this third-grade classroom, the teacher works with two different classes a day. So she created one "I Can" chart with the morning class on white paper. The chart on the green paper was made with her afternoon class. Both are displayed in the classroom library to remind students what they can do there.

Q: *Where do I put my math charts?*

A: You will probably want to create a special place to display your math charts. Many teachers have their large-group teaching area in a corner and use one wall for language arts and the other for math.

Calendar materials are displayed on the left and literacy on the right in this large-group teaching area.

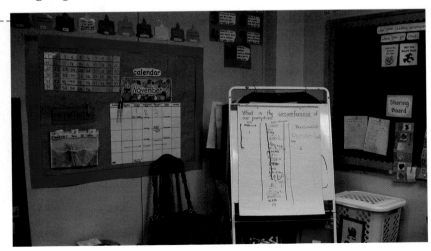

Sticky notes added to the clock help students learn to tell time. In essence, the clock now becomes a math "anchor chart."

Clocks posted on the chalkboard can be changed as needed to reflect the day's schedule. This type of anchor chart helps students know what to expect during the day.

Calendar math is displayed on part of a bulletin board in the whole-group teaching area.

Q: I don't have many walls. Where can I display things?

A: Use the few walls you DO have thoughtfully. And to extend your display area, post things on your cabinet doors and even windows. Some teachers hang clotheslines for extra display, too (only if in accordance with fire codes).

This kindergarten teacher posts tools (names chart, ABC chart, and writing samples) for students to use at the writing station on her window due to limited wall space. She places her writing table (covered with dry erase lined paper) by the window for a writing surface.

A word wall is made from paper attached to a clothesline in front of a window in first grade (and the fire marshal allows it).

This display is posted on a cabinet door because the teacher has no extra wall space. After she models how to use a graphic organizer in whole group well, the graphic is posted in a file folder with a smaller picture of it on the front. Copies of the graphic organizers are kept in each folder. Kids use these at a variety of literacy work stations, such as listening, buddy reading, and classroom library, for response.

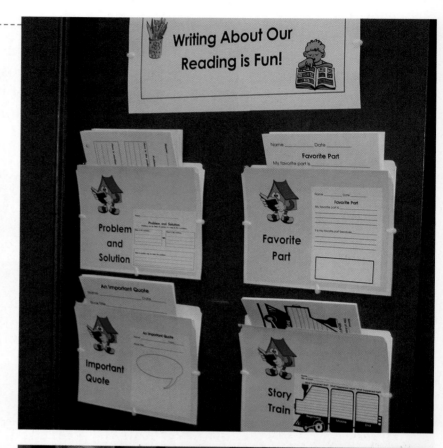

Students in this second-grade classroom put their ideas on sticky notes on a cabinet door in response to their work stations that day. The teacher uses these for assessment of how stations are going. The clear plastic shoe holder beside it holds desk supplies easily accessible to students for their independent use.

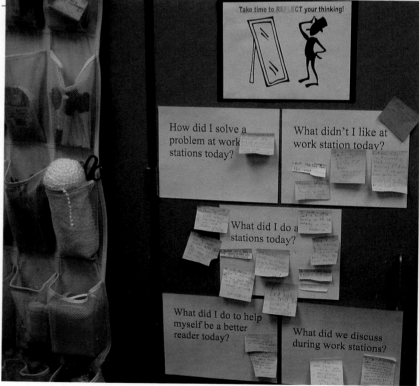

What About Word Walls?

What is the purpose of this space? How does it link to instruction? What materials will we need here?

Upper- and lowercase letters are displayed to help young children learn about letters and sounds and ABC order.

Vowels are in blue to make them stand out.

A few examples of environmental print, like *McDonald's* for *Mm*, will help kids learn letter names and sounds in pre-K and kindergarten.

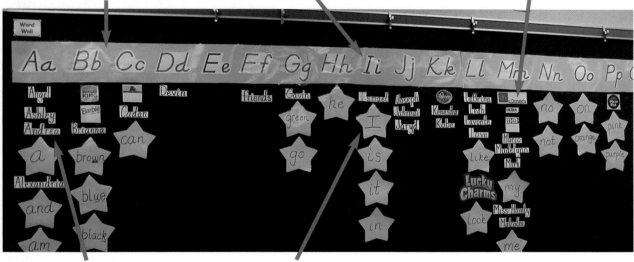

At the start of the year, add children's names to the wall to help them learn about print in pre-K, K, and first grade.

High-frequency words are written on star-shaped cards to make them stand out. These are words that are "starring" in young children's reading and writing. Add these as kids need to learn to read and write them. Once the words are on the wall, expect kids to spell them correctly.

This word wall is on a magnetic chalkboard and words are attached with magnetic tape to make it low and interactive.

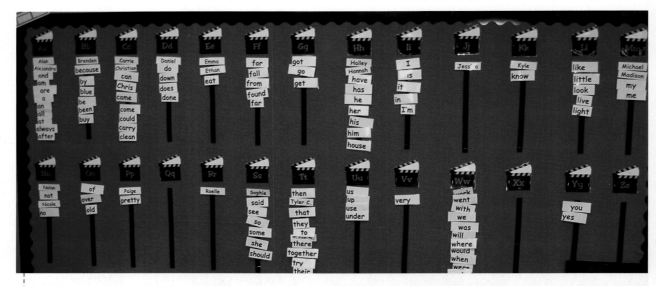

This first-grade word wall is on a large bulletin board covered with paper. Strips of magnetic tape are affixed to it. Words can be taken on and off the wall easily by the children, since the words have small bits of magnetic tape on them.

MY INSTRUCTION	SPACE I'LL NEED	THOUGHTS ON SETTING UP
teaching with my word wall rather than have it just be a display	word wall that is low and interactive for emergent and early readers and close to whole-group teaching space	• place it near whole-group teaching area to be able to make connections with word wall words while teaching shared reading and writing lessons • make it low and interactive in a pre-K through first-grade classroom (use part of my magnetic dry erase board in the front of the room)

OTHER THINGS YOU MIGHT LIKE HERE

ESSENTIALS/MUST-HAVES		LINK TO INSTRUCTION
Word Wall • cards with upper- and lowercase letters written on them (and picture cue for phonics in primary grades) • word wall words typed large enough (in black) for all students to see • low, interactive placement for students in pre-K, K, and grade 1 (so kids can see and reach words) • interesting words for vocabulary building in grades 2 and up • high-frequency words in pre-K through grade 1	**Word Wall** • shelves/stacking baskets for ABC/word study materials by the word wall • sorting space or large metal tray for sorts • place this near your ABC/word study station and your writing station, if possible, so kids can access these words	**Word Wall** • display for words we're paying attention to as readers and writers • make connections to these words while modeling how to read and write • use and spell these words correctly in your reading and writing throughout the day • in pre-K through grade 1, be able to take words on/off wall as you need them or want to explore them and how they relate to other words

This space-saving word wall is made with two tri-fold display boards pushed together. Phonics cards are used to name letters. Students' names and high-frequency words are fastened onto Velcro strips on the project board to make this word wall interactive. It can be moved from the whole-group teaching area to the small-group area or even used as an ABC/word study station during independent time.

First, this kindergarten teacher makes a names chart with the class. She writes one name at a time while kids tell what they notice about the letters. Then those same names are added to the word wall where they will be used during shared reading and writing to teach about letters and sounds. Magnetic tape is added to the back of each word wall word to attach it to the display.

This third-grade word wall grew from read-aloud and shared reading. Kids note interesting new words and help the teacher make cards to add to the wall. They are encouraged to use these words in their speaking, reading, and writing.

Here's another type of word wall—an interesting words wall from a fifth-grade classroom. This one is organized by parts of speech to help students with grammar and vocabulary.

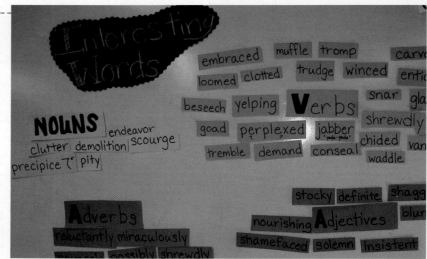

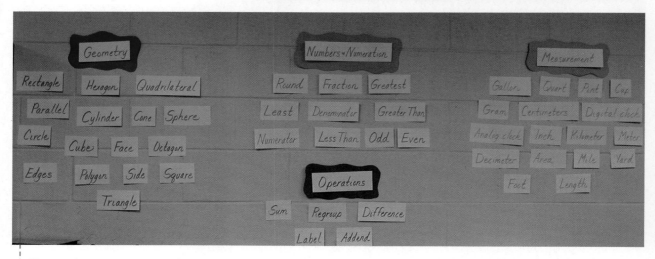

Key math terms are posted on this upper-grade math word wall, which is another kind of word wall.

KIND OF WORD WALL	WHAT TO DISPLAY THERE	WHERE TO GET THOSE WORDS	PURPOSE OF WORD WALL	APPROPRIATE GRADE LEVELS AND DISPLAY TIPS
high-frequency word wall	• high-frequency words (you want kids to read and write) • kids' names (and photos in pre-K and K)	• grade-level word list from your school/district/core program • words kids frequently must read and write at their reading level	• to learn to read and write high-frequency words to help with reading (and writing) fluency • to pay attention to print • to use their names to learn beginning (and ending) sounds and chunks	• pre-K, K, grade 1, start of grade 2 • organize in ABC order under the first letter of each word
interesting words wall	• higher-level vocabulary words you want kids to use in their speaking, reading, and writing	• "harvest" these words as you read aloud or do shared reading with the class	• to pay attention to new words and become a word detective (one who gathers and uses new words) • to expand vocabulary	• middle of grade 2 and up • organize in ABC order or by part of speech • kids can help make the cards for the wall
content-area word wall	• words clustered around a unit of study in science, social studies, or math	• new words important to that unit of study • see bold words in content-area textbooks	• to learn content-area vocabulary (and use it in speaking, reading, and writing) • to encourage students to spell these words correctly	• grade K and up • add photos (from the Internet) or illustrations

Q: Should I put my content words on the word wall?

A: You may choose to have a content-area word wall (math, science, social studies) or create content-area word charts instead. Cluster words from each unit of study together on your display. Don't mix content words and high-frequency words. It can confuse kids. NOTE: Content-area word charts will save you space.

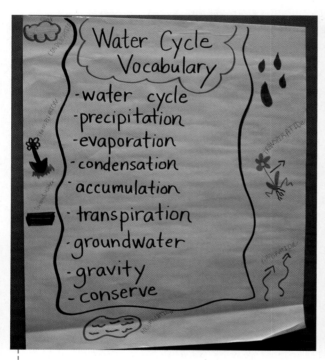

For each science unit, the teacher makes a vocabulary chart with the students (instead of putting these on a word wall). Kid-friendly definitions may be added with sticky notes. Students drew the illustrations in the margin to match the new words. Display this chart during the unit of study and refer to it while teaching. Encourage kids to use these words in their speaking, reading, and writing. At the end of the unit, put rings at the top of the chart and hang this on a chart stand for reference as needed. This example is from a fifth-grade science unit about the water cycle.

Science words are posted on cards and displayed on cabinet doors throughout the year in this upper-grade classroom.

Next Steps/Things to Try

1. Look at your walls. You might take digital photos of them, so you can take them out of your room and look at them more objectively. Which walls are working well? Why? Which ones aren't, and why? Get a colleague to help you look at your wall spaces and suggest ways to better utilize them, using ideas from this chapter.

2. Which walls do your students use the most in your room? Why? Which ones do they rarely use? Why do you think this is happening? What would you like to add to your walls? What can you edit?

3. Find a teacher you respect and trust for this activity. Plan to visit each other's rooms alone when there are no students present. While there, jot down what you think this teacher values by looking at his or her walls. Also make notes on display ideas, including compliments and suggestions. Then meet together and share your notes. Help each other.

4. Use the charts in this book to help you better utilize your wall space. What did you find most helpful? Share with a colleague.

5. Look at the colors in your displays, including bulletin board backgrounds and borders. How many different colors and patterns have you used? Look at the pictures in the chapter for inspiration. Try to pare down your color schemes to simple ones, using just 2 or 3 colors for consistency.

6. Meet with your grade-level team and have everyone bring some of the anchor charts they've been making with their classes. Share ideas, and discuss ways to display and store these using ideas from this chapter.

7. Look at your word wall if you use one. What is its purpose? How are you using it? What kinds of words are on it? Is it easy for students to access? Share word wall ideas with others at your grade level.

8. Where are you on this continuum for using your walls? Think about next steps you'd like to take.

1   2   3   4

1. My school requires we hang certain things on the walls. I also bought materials from a teacher supply store to decorate my walls and bulletin boards.

2. I don't usually think much about my walls from the kids' perspective. I put things up as I teach with them, but it's probably time to look more thoughtfully at this space.

Using Your Walls

3. My walls are next on my list of things to look at. I've gotten the rest of my room better organized, and now I'm ready to look at the walls. I hang up student work and charts we make. I like the idea of looking at colors and borders and thinking about what kids really use that's on the walls.

4. I'm going to really look carefully at what I have and put on my walls. Some of this stuff has been hanging up all year, and it's time to edit. I'll only display what is useful and important to me and my class. I might take photos of my walls, so I can look objectively at what's on them.

Chapter 5

Organizing Your Stuff

Packing
Moving
Storing

One of the most frequent questions I get is about where to put all our stuff. We teachers have so many materials and often there is very limited storage space. One school hired me to help two veteran teachers sort through their materials. They had both just received many new resources from a grant, but were having trouble using the new things due to the fact that they had so much stuff. As we examined what was taking up space on their shelves, we found things from as far back as the 1960s that were just gathering dust. So, we got a large trash can and several extra bags and got to work. Most of us can benefit from a good weeding out yearly.

When we only keep what we plan to teach with *this year* in our classrooms, it seems to also declutter our minds and help us think about current teaching methods and ideas. When we store all we've used in our teaching from every year we've ever taught, we run out of room and have trouble making space for new ideas. Here are some of the items I've helped folks part with over the years:

155

- purple ditto masters
- kits dating back 15 to 30 years
- antique reading books (collectibles that might be displayed at home)
- materials made in college (from 5 to 15 years ago) that took too long to make and kids don't like using
- puzzles and games with missing pieces
- half-empty containers with contents that can be consolidated and take up less space
- extra art supplies that could be donated to needy schools or families

Not long ago, I had the pleasure of helping a couple of teachers at the end of the year. I helped Patty reorganize her storage areas to make the following start of the year a breeze. Her friend Sara was moving to a new school, and I helped her develop a method for packing that I hope will be helpful to you should you find yourself in this situation. Both systems involved using labels, a simple tool that can transform storage spaces. This chapter begins with these step-by-step ideas for packing and moving.

By request, it also contains ideas for easy and innovative ways to store things in your classroom. Finally, this chapter ends by showing how we transformed one teacher's storage area and helped her find valuable space for her students and their work. I've included bits of our conversation to help guide you as you look at your spaces for storage.

As I've deeply examined the concept of storage, I've learned that there is always enough room for the things we value. When we get our spaces under control, we feel more in control, too. A well-organized classroom can result in a well-managed classroom.

So pick a space that's been bugging you. Grab a trash can and some extra garbage bags and get to work. If you're like me and have trouble throwing things away, get a friend (who's good at throwing things away) to help you. Find places for all the important stuff, and ultimately, you'll create more space for your students!

A Simple System for Packing and Storing

We look forward to the end of school and summertime. But there's that job of putting everything away until next year. And where do you store all that stuff? How do you quickly and easily take down bulletin boards, pack up materials, and stow it all for the summer? Do you jam it in the closets, hoping it will all fit? Do you have a place for everything and everything in its place?

Part One: The Last Weeks at School with Kids

Continue to teach until the last day at school.

Don't take your room apart before then. It gives kids the message that learning is over. And this can make the last week of school crazy! Continue to teach in your room in a structured learning environment. Kids will be happy, and so will you.

But I'll never get everything packed in a day!

Yes, you will . . . if you have a system for putting things away in your room. An organized classroom (inside and out) will facilitate the packing process. See the "Storing" section of this chapter for ideas.

--- **MAY/JUNE** ---

MONDAY	TUESDAY	WEDNESDAY	THURSDAY	FRIDAY
25 Begin to write class play together. Include enough parts for all kids to have one.	**26** Extra read-aloud starts today— choose chapter book in a series kids may enjoy for summer reading	**27** Write book reviews for summer books.	**28** Tryouts for class play.	**29** Poetry party today. We all read and share favorite poems.
1 Play practice starts today.	**2** Play practice continues.	**3** Perform class play. Use scripts if needed. It's the end of school, and that's okay!	**4** LAST DAY FOR KIDS	**5** TEACHER WORK DAY

Packing

What can I do after the office collects all my books?

In many schools, the office must do an end-of-the-year inventory of all state-issued textbooks. So they collect these teaching materials several weeks before school ends. Here are some things to try when your books have been gathered up:

1. You still have classroom library books. Teach with those. Use them for read-alouds. Do shared writing of book reviews with your class. Have kids make summer reading recommendations for each other.
2. Continue to teach with literacy stations and small-group instruction. Nobody has taken away your furniture! If you don't have little books for small-group reading, use copies of poetry for a change, or reader's theater scripts or news articles.
3. Do something you had trouble finding time for during the regular school year. I used to write a play with my class and act it out the last week of school. The children put all their energy into reading the script, trying out for parts, and practicing for the big performance. We performed for other classes and for parents who could attend.

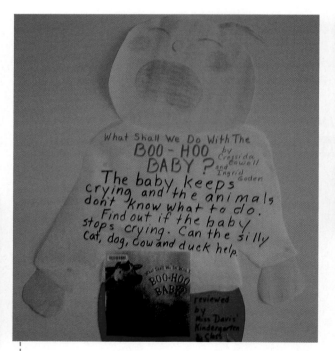

A sample summer book review is written with the class as shared writing following read-aloud. Copies of book reviews might be sent home with a summer reading list.

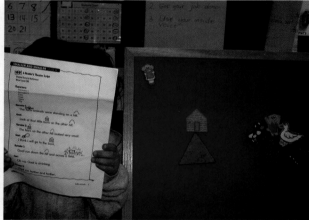

Students read reader's theater script and act out story on a flannelboard at the drama station.

On the last day of school, get the kids to help you take things down and put them away.

A student removes sentence strips for the pocket chart station from a bulletin board.

Sentence strips are stored in storage box from teacher supply store. Sort strips month by month, organizing them from easiest to more challenging. Label each box with the months for the sentence strips stored inside. Pocket chart is stored on top of the boxes in a cabinet designated for literacy materials.

A child takes out photos and icons from this year's literacy stations management board (made from a pocket chart).

A student helper gives each child his or her photo from the management board to take home as a memento.

Packing

Kids pack up books to take home for summer reading.

Students help put away little leveled books from small-group reading instruction in labeled baskets.

Part Two: After the Kids Have Left

Empty one space at a time and sort through it. Just ONE space at a time!

Ask Yourself: Should I Keep This?

- Have I used it this year?
- Do I want to use it next year?
- Is this something I might look over and use this summer to improve my teaching next year?
- Do I already have a copy of this?
- Does this belong to my school system? Or is it mine?
- I used to use this, but I have something better to use now.

Stay focused. Sort one space at a time. Don't leave this space to put anything away. If you do, you may get distracted and try to start cleaning up that space! You'll probably find that if you are successful with one space, you'll eagerly tackle another.

Things You'll Need When Sorting Through Your Stuff

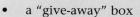

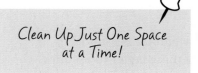

Clean Up Just One Space at a Time!

- a "give-away" box
- a large trash can
- extra trash bags
- a friend who's good at throwing away things (if this is difficult for you)

When things are labeled, it will be easy for you to put them away . . . daily as well as at the end of the year.

Store all your literacy work stations supplies in one area. Label everything. This is what the teacher had left after we sorted through all her stuff. She makes most of her teaching materials with students during the year, so there isn't much to store.

- Use clear plastic shoeboxes to store materials for easy retrieval. You can actually SEE what's in them.
- Place materials for each literacy station in a separate container.
- Add large mailing labels (restickable kind) to help you find what you need and put things back where they belong.

If getting organized seems like an overwhelming task, get a friend to help you throw things away.
Less stuff = less stress

If You're Moving . . .

It's the end of the year. Or maybe it's partway through, and you must move for some reason:

- *new carpet being installed in your classroom*
- *your principal has asked you to move to a new grade level*
- *a job transfer*

If you're like most of us, you just throw things in boxes to get them packed quickly. But there is a better way that will save you time in the long run.

How do you pack all your things and easily retrieve them at the start of the next year or your next job? If you'd like to make packing up your room simple, read on.

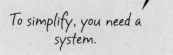

To simplify, you need a system.

Classroom Library Before Moving

Classroom Library Materials Packed

Classroom library books in labeled storage boxes (left)

Pillows and baskets in giant, clear Ziploc bags (right)

Moving

Step One:	Start the packing process by MAKING A PLAN:

1. Take inventory of what you've got. Ask yourself . . .
   a. "What belongs to me?"
   b. "What is owned by the school?" (and must stay in this room)
2. Make a list of what you will move (that belongs to you).
   a. Look at big categories, such as books, literacy materials, math materials, files, etc. (see Sara's sample "Packing Up to Move" list)
   b. Don't get bogged down noting every little thing you'll be taking.
3. Create a list of packing materials needed. (see sample list following)
   a. Include measurements of what you'll need to pack, such as sizes of books (professional and children's).
   b. List everything you can think of (so you can stay focused on the packing task and not have to run off to find things).
   c. Estimate numbers of boxes, labels, etc., to save time.

> "Failing to plan is planning to fail."
> —Alan Lakein

Sara's List of What to Move

Packing Up to Move
- books
  - children's books including fiction and nonfiction
  - professional books
- literacy work stations stuff
  - ABC/word study materials
  - science and social studies things used at stations
  - writing stations stuff
  - Big Book stuff
  - poetry charts and pointers
  - listening materials
  - overhead stuff
  - games and puzzles
- teacher office stuff and art supplies
- math stuff
  - games and stuff
  - math work stations stuff
- refrigerator
- files

Must Do
- separate school stuff from my stuff
- separate early-in-the-year stuff from later-in-the-year stuff
- clean out file cabinets as best as possible, so I don't have to move all those files
- Ask: "What can I easily part with?"

Sara's List of Packing Materials

- cardboard boxes from Office Depot (for books)—3 boxes plus 1 box for art supplies)
- must hold boxes 12 inches high by 4 ½ inches wide by 10 inches deep (with books in them)—take an empty box along—30 book boxes must fit in containers—look for clear container
- Ziploc bags (assorted sizes)
- stick-on labels—large mailing size
- index card box with A–Z dividers for word wall words
- large clear bags for plastic containers (garbage size, not black)
- 4 or 5 clear plastic shoeboxes for teacher office stuff
- 1 large box for big teacher charts from teacher supply store
- clear packing tape
- scissors
- black marker for labeling
- photos printed of classroom spaces
- tote to hold all supplies for my "packing kit"

Moving

large labels for storage boxes listing what's in each

ruler for measuring books and other items needing to be packed

Ziploc bags for packing small items

plastic ties for securing hangers used in poetry station

Organizer

basket to carry around packing supplies so you don't lose them

Packing Kit

Moving

| Step Two: | On another day, prepare for moving by TAKING PHOTOS. |

Step Two:

On another day, prepare for moving by TAKING PHOTOS.

- Take photos of spaces in your classroom that are working. Be sure to capture all materials you'll be packing in each photo.
- Print your photos on 8½-by-11-inch paper in full color. If you will need more than one box to pack your items for an area, duplicate that photo for as many boxes as needed.

The ABC/Word Study Station is pictured above. We took this photo and then copied it onto 8½-by-11-inch paper and glued it to the packing box (right) with all the materials needed for this station stored inside.

8½-by-11-inch photo of materials stored inside this box, taped to box with clear packing tape

mailing address label tells what's in the box

And now . . .

a word about file cabinets.

Just how many file folders do you really need?

Ask Yourself . . .

- How many filing cabinets do I currently have in my room?
- How many will I have in my new space? How many filing cabinets do I really need?
- Could I condense what I take with me to 1 or 2 filing cabinets?

> Plan to go through your files a month or so before packing and moving days. Quickly make decisions about what's important for your current teaching job.

Section off your files into groups of about 30 or 40 a day to weed through.

Label each section with the day you will look at this section of files.

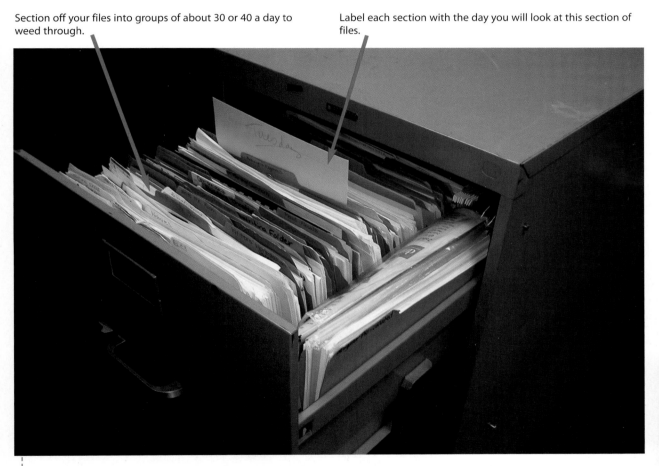

- Divide your overcrowded file cabinet into manageable sections, as pictured above. Give yourself a week or two to go through them all.
- It took years to create this clutter. Take a few weeks to conquer it.

Moving

Get rid of:

- extra copies of things. You need only *one* copy of each.
  - Draw a line at the top of your "master copy" with a yellow highlighter and keep it. Throw the extras away.
  - Next year make copies from it and then return it to its folder home.
- purple ditto masters (yes, some teachers *still* have these hidden in filing cabinets).
- outdated memos and papers.
  - We often put these in files thinking we'll need them some-time this year. The year is over; put them in the recycle bin!
- files related to grade levels other than the one you'll be teaching next.
  - Store these in a different-colored folder in a separate box marked "Files for other grade levels."
  - Take them home (not to your new school) to store so they don't clutter up your new teaching space.
- things you haven't used this year (unless they're so good you want to use them next year, but just forgot about this year since your files were so overcrowded).
- records for this year's students.
  - Put these aside to give to the office for students' cumulative files.

When in Doubt, Throw It Out

Step Three:

pictured on the following page.

Gather storage containers for moving.
- First, look at what you've already got. No shopping yet!
- Consider clear plastic storage bins, baskets, totes, etc. Many of us find all kinds of containers we'd bought on previous organizing attempts.
  - You'll need containers of varying sizes.
  - Those with lids are most useful for moving.
- Store containers without lids in large, clear Ziploc bags, like those pictured on the following page.
- I like to use strong cardboard storage boxes or boxes in which paper is sold. Grocery store boxes often break when moving them and can be awkward to transport.
- Allow yourself one large teacher storage box. Only one!!! You don't need all that "big stuff." It takes up too much valuable space.

MOVING TIP: **Slow down to speed up.** Organizing **before** you move will make setting up your new place a breeze. Slowing down (and thoughtfully packing) will help you speed up (as you unpack with ease) in your new space.

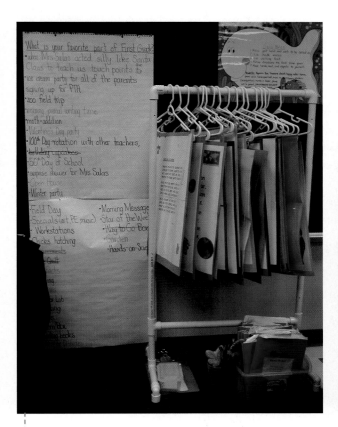

Big charts need to be packed.

One large teacher storage box holds big charts (available from teacher supply store).

Moving

Large, clear Ziploc bags are perfect for storing large items like pillows and baskets without lids.

They are clear so you can SEE what's stored in them!

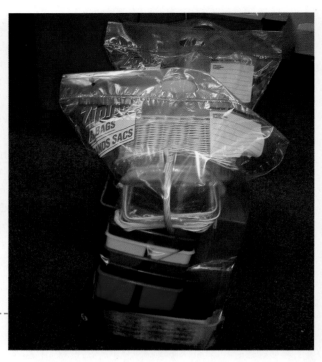

Step Four:	Prepare your boxes and moving containers.

- Fasten each 8½-by-11-inch photo onto the box in which you'll put materials used in that area.
- Attach a large mailing label, too, and write the name of the space on it.
- Stack your boxes in a corner or on a countertop away from your teaching space.

boxes ready for files to keep and move

only one large box for charts and over-sized items to move

Moving

Step Five: The last day of school, have the students help you take things down and put them in labeled boxes.

Kids take down literacy work stations signs and management board pieces.

They store the pieces in a Ziploc bag along with a photo of the management board.

Step Six: Pack your boxes. Place them by the door. Call a friend and move them to your next teaching home.

This is all Sara has that must be moved. The entire contents of her room are ready to be transferred to her new school. Sara told me afterward, "This was so easy. I can't believe how little I *really* need to teach well with. I am keeping the boxes to store things in at the end of the year, too."

Moving

Storing Suggestions

Here are some ideas for interesting, inexpensive ways to store things for back-to-school time:

Clip-on job tags are kept in a small plastic basket. They match the helpers chart and are worn by students to show their jobs.

A wooden tray atop a student desk holds name tags, bus tags, and other back-to-school paraphernalia for the first days of school.

When cleaning up at the end of the year, we found items we needed for the next year and placed them in a special drawer, labeled "Back to School." It holds a new lesson plan book, blank name tags, paper strips for bus tags, etc.

This plastic container labeled "Sub Tub" holds materials for a substitute, including sub plans, a seating chart, special notes for subs, and materials needed for a day when the teacher is out. It is stored on the teacher's desk in plain view.

More Storage Ideas

This basket holds books kids find that need repaired in their classroom library.

A crate holding handwriting supplies is labeled to let students know what is in this portable space-saving station. They carry it to a desk for independent practice.

Letter cards for making words activities are stored in trays recycled from frozen diet meals. Each tray holds multiples of the card on top.

Math manipulatives are stored in stacking plastic candy jars. A sample of the material is hot-glued on the lid to show what's inside.

Storing

An accordion file holds transparencies for kids to use independently at this overhead work station. The label tells children what's inside.

Word wall cards and alphabet cards to organize the wall are stored in a plastic index card file. Cards are filed in alphabetical order to keep them organized at the end of the year.

Materials for this pocket chart station are stored on the side of a file cabinet. Each set of materials (pictures and names, cards for ABC order, and consonant cards for matching beginning sounds) are kept in Ziploc bags and attached to the cabinet with bulldog clips on magnets. Another couple of strong magnetic hooks hold sentence strips and a pointer. The pocket chart is tacked low on a bulletin board to make it easily accessible to kids.

Storing

A tape/CD player and music are stored in back of the Big Book easel in this kindergarten classroom in the whole-group teaching area for easy access. Extra CDs are stored in a basket nearby.

Cubes made with metal grids that link together create great open storage for teacher supplies in the teacher desk area.

Creation station materials are stored in stacking drawers and individual baskets, which are labeled to help them stay organized. A three-ring note-book with clear plastic sleeves holds step-by-step instructions for simple projects students can make here.

Storing

We met Heather in the "Using Your Walls" chapter. Now watch her storage-area transformation.

Storage: BEFORE

Heather is using her counter-tops for storage space and losing valuable wall display room. On the left side of the counter, she stores picture books and professional books inside shelves, because she doesn't know where else to put them. To the right, she has paper stored in old cardboard sorting trays.

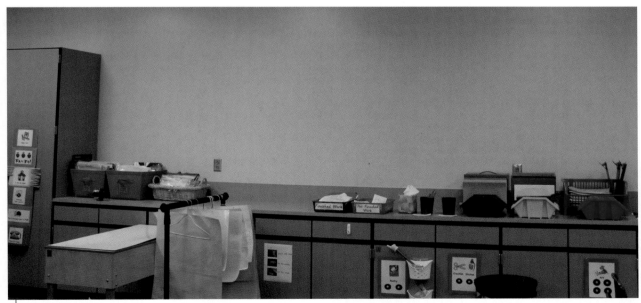

Storage: AFTER

We worked together to create new places to store all the materials she had kept on top of her counters. This gave us much-needed wall space for displays of student work that can now be added.

Storing

So . . . Where Did You Put All Her Stuff?

We went through each set of items, one at a time, systematically, to decide what to keep and where to store it. Here's our plan and some snippets from our conversation:

Step One: Paper Storage

PROBLEM	SOLUTION
• Dead space on paper storage shelves • Old cardboard shelves falling apart	• Use clear acrylic paper sorters for paper storage and red basket for notebooks and clipboards

Debbie: This paper storage unit has lots of dead space. How attached are you to it?

Heather: I've had it for 8 years. I bought it my first year of teaching because I couldn't afford anything else. I'm okay with getting rid of it. It's falling apart.

Debbie: There are some clear plastic paper organizers from the office supply store that will take up much less space, and you have some containers we can use to store other art materials here, too.

Heather: Wow! I can't believe how much better this looks. The kids will love it. Now they can get paper, writing books, clipboards, and special scissors here. And it hardly takes up any space.

Paper is stored BEFORE in ramshackle cardboard trays (purchased 8 years ago when she started to teach). Lots of "dead space" is not being used, which covers up the walls.

AFTER: Construction paper storage is now in two clear plastic sorting trays. Student notebooks are stored in red basket with clipboards handy for student use. Three small, colored containers in front hold scrap paper and fancy scissors for art projects that students can easily access.

Step Two:	Books on Countertop

PROBLEM	SOLUTION
• These bookshelves could be used by kids • Music materials and ABC tubs too far away from teaching areas to be used easily	• Find storage spots in cabinets for books and move bookshelves to classroom library for student use • Move music materials and ABC tubs to small-group teaching area • Weed through professional books and binders and move to teacher desk area

Debbie: Let's look at each item in these baskets and on these shelves. How do you use these materials?

Heather: Some of these professional materials I just don't use anymore. I have better books I've bought over the years. I can get rid of the ones I don't use. These are music materials I use for transitions. And these are some of my read-alouds that I have organized.

Debbie: Would it be okay to move some things to areas closer to where you'll use them? How about if we work to find space for these books inside your cabinets?

Heather: I'd love that. But I have all these art materials in my cabinets. And I don't think these blue baskets will fit. Where will we put the bookshelves?

Debbie: Let's try to consolidate the art stuff and get it all in one cabinet (instead of several). And let's move the shelves to your classroom library. You told me you were thinking about rearranging it anyway.

BEFORE: On the left are music materials and games in baskets. Read-aloud books are stored in the blue baskets by topic on top of the brown wooden bookshelf. Professional books and binders are stored on the bottom and top shelves.

BEFORE: Additional read-aloud books are stored in the blue and red bookshelves on top of the counter. ABC sorting tubs are placed on top of the red shelves. The long basket on top of the blue shelves holds birthday supplies.

Storing

AFTER: Author study books were moved to cabinets under counter. Rainy day games were also stored here (on bottom shelf). NOTE: Heather got rid of many items previously stored here. Some moved to a new, more convenient location; some were thrown away; and quite a few were taken home for a garage sale.

AFTER: Read-aloud books (previously on countertop) were moved to another set of shelves below the counter, too. Heather also cleaned out this space and consolidated materials that moved to new locations, as in picture on left.

AFTER: Red and blue bookshelves were moved to the classroom library to make room for more books for students to read here.

AFTER: Professional books and binders frequently used are now stored on the brown shelf, which was moved behind the teacher's small-group teaching area near her teacher desk. So were the ABC tubs.

Step Three:

Art Supplies

NOTE to upper-grade teachers: You may not have all these art supplies, but you may have another type of material that tends to overtake your storage areas, such as test-taking supplies.

PROBLEM	SOLUTION
• Too many art supplies being stored under counter in cabinets and shelves	• Donate extra supplies to charity • Throw away stuff nobody will ever use

Debbie: Do you use these plastic lids?

Heather: I thought they might be good for art projects, but I've never used them. Guess we can get rid of them?

Debbie: This glitter looks dried up. Do you really need three bags of cotton balls?

Heather: We can throw away the glitter. I'll donate some of these extra supplies to charity. We have way too many supplies. I'll never use them all. This tissue paper got wet and is of no use. I'll throw it away, too.

Debbie: Let's think about using these drawers for supplies we want kids to easily access. How about putting writing paper in here? We'll label the drawers so kids can find what they need on their own.

BEFORE: Art materials are stored in cabinet under counters. Too much stuff!

BEFORE: Paper plates, pipe cleaners, watercolors, and extra pencils are kept in drawers right under counter.

AFTER: All art materials were consolidated in one cabinet. Storage tubs were found as we threw stuff away.

AFTER: Drawers hold "kid paper" in them for writing. Labels on the front of drawers will help kids help themselves.

Storing

Step Four: The Cabinets and Closets

PROBLEM	SOLUTION
• Things not used in many years are stored here	• Ruthlessly look at each item and decide if it stays and where to put it that is logical, easy to access, and safe
• Sometimes excess stuff is stored here	• Dispose of things no longer used
	• Donate extra supplies to charity
	• Take some things home for garage sale

Debbie: Your closets are organized well. You have one closet for math and another for literacy. What would you like to change?

Heather: I'd like to be able to more easily get to some of my materials, like my math manipulatives. And some of these storage containers are breaking.

Debbie: I saw another teacher store her read-aloud books in magazine boxes. Would you be interested in trying that?

Heather: Yes, in fact I have a bunch of them at home.

Debbie: Let's move these Ziploc bags to a drawer. I think you'll have much easier access to them.

Heather: (*after moving them*) This is just like my kitchen at home! I love it!

BEFORE: Math manipulatives stored in large stacking drawers in closet are hard to open. Ziploc bags are crammed beside these and are hard to access.

BEFORE: Books for read-aloud are stored in baskets stacked on top of each other. This system is organized but takes up lots of space.

AFTER: Read-aloud books moved from crates into magazine boxes take up much less space. Labels help quickly identify what's where.

AFTER: Math manipulatives were stored in sturdier stacking drawers labeled for easy access. Storytelling boards are now stored where Ziploc bags were stacked before. We ran out of magazine boxes, but Heather will consolidate the last blue basket (on bottom shelf) into those later.

Throwing away old stuff you no longer use—even if it took you forever to make—creates space for items you use.

The end result makes happy, purposeful teachers who can teach more easily because they can easily get their fingertips on what they need quickly.

Next Steps/Things to Try

PACKING: (This discussion will probably work best as you approach the last month of school or before a move you must make.)

1. Talk with your colleagues. What has worked well for you in past years as you've packed up at the end of the year? What new tips did you get from this chapter? What will you try?

2. Also discuss what you'll do with your students during the last two weeks of school this year. Share ideas with your team. Brainstorm ideas of what you can do when the school collects many of the school's materials for inventory.

3. Plan how you'll involve your students to help you with packing (and/or moving). Think of the system you'll use to effectively and efficiently pack up your room so it's ready to use next year.

4. Take some time to reflect on this past year. What worked well? What areas worked best? What materials were effective? What didn't work so well? What can you get rid of?

5. If you're moving, what will you try from this chapter? Even if you're not moving this year, what ideas did you like from this section?

STORING: (Use these ideas when you decide to reorganize any storage area in your room.)

6. The end of December/early January and the end of the school year are both good times to look at your classroom space, especially storage areas. What areas are overcrowded and need weeding?

7. Choose *one* space in your classroom to begin sorting through. Use the suggestions from this chapter to help you make decisions about what to keep and what to get rid of. If you haven't used it, don't keep it in your room. Get a friend to help you (who is good at getting rid of stuff)! Note: Don't buy storage containers before you start to organize. Buy them only when you find out what you need that fits your space.

8. Where are you on this continuum for storing materials? Think about next steps you'd like to take.

```
1 ◄───────── 2 ───────── 3 ───────── 4 ─────────►
```

1. I wish I had more space in my classroom. There's just nowhere to store all my stuff. I can't throw things away. I might need them someday.

2. I don't have time to think about cleaning up my cabinets. I barely have time to do my lesson plans. But it would help if I could get my desk cleaned up. I'll use ideas from this chapter to help me with that.

3. I've been wanting to redo my storage area, especially my cabinets. During the break, I'll make that a priority and get started.

4. I realize that I must start with my storage spaces if I want to find room for all that's important in my classroom. I'm going to start with one storage space at a time and clean it out after school. There are probably lots of things I no longer need. If I just take one shelf a day, I'll be able to have this done in a few weeks.

9. Invite colleagues to see your newly organized spaces. Your work will most likely inspire others. Celebrate your successes. Go to a movie, read a good book, or take a long walk. Do something fun. Most likely, you'll gain some free time as the result of your newly organized space. Enjoy!

Resources

Where to
Find It

Chapter 1—Planning Your Space

p. 21

- wire locker baskets from www.stacksandstacks.com and www.spacesavers.com

p. 25

- Lego block table and Community Play Carpet from Lakeshore Learning
- shower board available at building supply stores such as Home Depot and Lowe's
- So-Real Kitchen Units housekeeping furniture from Kaplan Early Learning at www.kaplanco.com

p. 26

- PVC pipe (P-trap) available from hardware stores or Whisper Phone from www.whisperphone.com

p. 28

- tri-fold project display boards from office supply stores

p. 29

- rug from Lowe's
- Soft Seats pillows from Lakeshore Learning
- Jumbo Pushpins from Wal-Mart
- three-stacking drawer units from Target
- All-Purpose Teacher's Organizer from Lakeshore Learning (pictured below pegboard)

p. 32

- magnetic poetry kit (on front of desk) from www.magneticpoetry.com
- plastic visor from dollar stores

p. 33

- white wooden bookshelves from Lowe's

Chapter 2—Arranging Your Room

p. 40

- rug from Lowe's

p. 41

- white wooden bookshelves from Lowe's
- folding children's chairs from Wal-Mart on clearance

p. 42

- 9-by-12-inch magnetic flexible sheets from www.ellison.com (used for word wall strips) and adhered with Scotch Mounting Squares to the wall
- stacking paper trays from office supply stores

p. 43

- interlocking plastic shelving (available in white) from www.qvc.com

p. 45

- furniture movers from hardware stores
- ClosetMaid 4 Tier Rolling Cart available at www.amazon.com

p. 47

- rug from Lowe's

p. 49

- white bookshelves from Home Depot
- folding chairs from Target on clearance
- dollar store baskets for book storage

p. 50

- shower board or marker board from Lowe's
- stools, storage containers, and lamp from Target

p. 52

- white plastic stacking shelves from Lowe's or Home Depot
- containers from dollar stores
- rug from Wal-Mart

p. 53
- magnetic paint and chalkboard paint from hardware and hobby stores

p. 55
- Classroom Mapping Tool from Debbie Diller Designs at Really Good Stuff

p. 57
- Magnetic Write and Wipe Board from Lakeshore Learning

p. 58
- headphone splitter from Radio Shack for CD player (to attach two headphones)
- Lakeshore Learning coffee mug used as pencil holder was free at back-to-school promotion

p. 59
- Leap Frog Fridge Phonics from Target, Wal-Mart, Kohl's, etc.
- word-sorting materials from *All Sorts of Sorts* by Sheron Brown from Teaching Resource Center at www.trcabc.com

p. 60
- drawer units for storing small parts from hardware stores
- student newspapers from Weekly Reader at www.weeklyreader.com or Scholastic News at www.scholasticnews.com

p. 61
- 5-pocket space-saving pocket charts from many school supply companies
- magnetic paint, chalkboard paint, and dry erase paint from hardware stores

p. 63
- housekeeping furniture from Wood Etc. at www.woodetccorp.com
- stacking baskets from Wal-Mart
- All-Purpose Teacher's Organizer from Lakeshore Learning (pictured in lower-left corner on table; also pictured on p. 86)

Chapter 3—Come On In!

p. 68
- writing chart stand easel from Office Depot
- rug from Lowe's
- Royal Reading/Writing Center from many school suppliers online (also pictured on p. 69)

p. 71
- Magnetic Write and Wipe Board and magnetic timer from Lakeshore Learning (also shown on p. 72)
- paint-can lids (by easel)—used for magnetic letter work
- pencil container from dollar stores

p. 72
- Sort & Store Book Organizer (for storing guided reading books in small-group area) from Lakeshore Learning
- file folder organizer from office supply stores

p. 73
- sturdy storage box from Lakeshore Learning
- Magnetic Word Builders from Lakeshore Learning
- Boone Rewritables dry erase markers at office supply stores

p. 74
- three-drawer stacking units from Target

p. 75
- teacher-made vowel charts made from laminated construction paper

p. 76
- wooden bookshelves from Home Depot

p. 78
- animal print rug from Target
- 1-inch book rings for fastening labels to baskets from office supply stores
- label pictures from images.google.com

p. 79
- child-size folding camp chairs from sporting good stores

p. 80
- clear plastic book containers from Lakeshore Learning
- rain gutter supplies from hardware stores
- inflatable pool and child-size lawn chairs from end-of-season clearance at drugstores

p. 81
- umbrella and folding chairs from Linens 'N Things
- rug from Home Depot
- indoor-outdoor carpet from Home Depot
- white plastic shelves, planters, lamps, picket fence, and tables from Home Depot
- plastic cable ties (used to fasten picket fence to back of shelves) from hardware stores

p. 84
- pumpkin, tabletop mirror, and plastic utensil tote from dollar stores
- stacking paper trays from office supply stores

p. 85
- Instant Activity Center from Lakeshore Learning (also pictured on p. 86)

- pencil container and plastic tablecloth from dollar stores
- basket hanging from chalk ledge from Wal-Mart

p. 86
- pegboard and pegboard hardware kits from hardware stores (also pictured on p. 87)
- All-Purpose Teacher Organizer from Lakeshore Learning (on table at top)
- Magnetic Display Clips from Lakeshore Learning
- folding stools from Wal-Mart

p. 88
- tri-fold project display board from office supply stores
- pencil chairs from end-of-season clearance at Walgreen's

p. 89
- library pockets from library suppliers (or ask your media specialist)

p. 91
- Bretford Connections Instruction Center for displaying computers and TV or printer on top from www.bretford.com

p. 92
- Elements of Reading vocabulary charts from Steck Vaughn at www.steckvaughn.com
- tackle box for magnetic letters from hardware or sporting goods stores
- Wikki Stix from school suppliers

p. 93
- stacking drawer wheeled cart from Wal-Mart
- automotive drip pan from auto supply stores (for magnetic letter work)

p. 94

- mirrors from dollar stores
- speech charts borrowed from school speech pathologist
- teacher-made portable word study station from large brown envelope, magnetic letters, and dry erase markers
- Write and Wipe Answer Boards (pictured in top picture in far-right container) from Lakeshore Learning

p. 95

- big purple flower in corner was a gift from a student
- Task Cards for Literacy Work Stations by Debbie Diller from Teaching Resource Center at www.trcabc.com

p. 96

- Jumbo Pushpins from Wal-Mart
- fluency rubric can be found in the *Fluency Rubric* Close-Up video by Debbie Diller from Stenhouse Publishers

p. 97

- highlighter tape available from school suppliers
- magnetic bulldog clip from Wal-Mart

p. 98

- large plastic laundry hamper from dollar stores
- suction cup clear plastic shower containers from Bed, Bath, and Beyond or Linens 'N Things

p. 100

- teacher-made desktop pocket chart made with PVC pipe
- colored macaroni glued onto small sentence strip pieces (To dye macaroni, place in Ziploc bag with 2 capfuls alcohol and 1 tube food coloring and shake to coat. Then dry on newspaper overnight.)

- names activities for work stations from *Beyond the Names Chart* by Debbie Diller from Teaching Resource Center (also on p. 99)
- environmental prints from students' homes

p. 102

- low overhead cart made by parent volunteer

p. 103

- wire cube storage unit available at Target, Wal-Mart, Home Depot, etc.

p. 104

- stacking baskets from Wal-Mart
- plastic visors and baskets from dollar stores

p. 105

- tri-fold project display board from office supply stores

p. 106

- puppet theater pictured is discontinued, but the Royal Puppet Theater from www.reallygoodstuff.com is a good substitute

p. 107

- chair pockets (not pictured) are a good space-saving alternative for student storage—check out the Happi-Pocket Chair Bag from www.chairbag.com

p. 109

- storage caddy from dollar stores

p. 111

- magnetic desk organizer from Wal-Mart and office supply stores

Chapter 4—Using Your Walls

Chapter 5—Organizing Your Stuff

- Ziploc Brand Big Bags size XXL from grocery stores (also pictured on p. 170 and 172)

p. 166
- plastic cable ties from hardware stores for packing kit
- magnetic chip clip (for attaching papers to magnetic spaces like side of file cabinet, pictured) from grocery stores

p. 169
- File 'n Save System Chart Storage Box from Target, www.restockit.com, and www.paper.com
- teacher-made chart stand made from PVC pipe

p. 173
- clip-on name tags from office supply stores

p. 174
- leftover trays from diet meals such as Lean Cuisine (for storing letter cards for making words) from grocery stores
- plastic stacking penny candy jars from promotional suppliers (in bulk) or leftover from snacks bought in these containers

p. 175
- accordion file folders from office supply stores
- magnetic bulldog clips from Wal-Mart

p. 176
- wire cube storage unit available at Target, Wal-Mart, Home Depot, etc.

p. 178
- acrylic vertical paper storage units from Wal-Mart and Office Depot
- blue, yellow, and red containers from Lakeshore Learning

pp. 179 and 180
- Alphabet Sounds Teaching Tubs from Lakeshore Learning

p. 183
- magazine storage boxes from IKEA at www.ikea.com

Resources

Reproducible Forms

Use the following at the end of each chapter to reflect on where you are and next steps you'd like to take.

Chapter 1

Planning My Space: My Continuum

$$\longleftarrow \quad 1 \qquad\qquad 2 \qquad\qquad 3 \qquad\qquad 4 \quad \longrightarrow$$

1. Just happy to have my room set up. Put things where they seem to fit. Using all kinds of colors. I might have too much furniture, and I might not have enough.
2. Realizing some areas of my room aren't well planned. Some areas get cluttered. Not sure what to do with it, though.
3. My room needs some reorganization. I'm going to choose one area and use ideas from this chapter to tackle it.
4. I'm working with a friend to reevaluate my entryway and how my whole space works for instruction. We are going to work together to make a map. First, I'm jotting down what's important to me. I'm making a thoughtful plan for space.

Chapter 2

Arranging My Room: My Continuum

$$\longleftarrow \quad 1 \qquad\qquad 2 \qquad\qquad 3 \qquad\qquad 4 \quad \longrightarrow$$

1. I didn't arrange my furniture. It was like this when I moved into my room. OR, I've always set up my room like this. I'm kind of used to it. OR, I change my room around constantly. I can't seem to find a way it works for me.
2. There are some parts of my room that aren't working so well. I'll ask my literacy coach or another teacher to help me pinpoint where to start.
3. I'm going to rethink my _____ teaching space. I'll choose several ideas from this book and my conversations with colleagues and kids to help me improve it.
4. I'm going to look critically at how we use space in our classroom. Next time I set it up, I'm using the order described in this book. For now, I'm going to watch to see how my kids are using the space. Then I'll fine-tune spaces using ideas from this chapter.

Spaces & Places: Designing Classrooms for Literacy by Debbie Diller. www.debbiediller.com. Copyright © 2008. Stenhouse Publishers.

Chapter 3

Thinking About All the Areas in My Room, Space by Space: My Continuum

| | 1 | 2 | 3 | 4 |

1. I never thought about my room, area by area, like in this chapter. It was just my classroom.
2. I'll pick one area and start there. I'll read the section on that space and then work on setting it up to work more effectively.
3. I've tried to set up different areas in my classroom. Now I'll fine-tune one or two of them. I will get a colleague to help me think through my space.
4. I'm going to look at each area in this chapter, systematically, and think about my space. I'll start with what's working well and try to identify what's making it work. Then I'll move onto other areas and work with them, one at a time.

Chapter 4

Using My Walls: My Continuum

| | 1 | 2 | 3 | 4 |

1. My school requires we hang certain things on the walls. I also bought materials from a teacher supply store to decorate my walls and bulletin boards.
2. I don't usually think much about my walls from the kids' perspective. I put things up as I teach with them, but it's probably time to look more thoughtfully at this space.
3. My walls are next on my list of things to look at. I've gotten the rest of my room better organized, and now I'm ready to look at the walls. I hang up student work and charts we make. I like the idea of looking at colors and borders and thinking about what kids really use that's on the walls.
4. I'm going to really look carefully at what I have and put on my walls. Some of this stuff has been hanging up all year, and it's time to edit. I'll only display what is useful and important to me and my class. I might take photos of my walls, so I can look objectively at what's on them.

Reproducible Forms

Chapter 5

Organizing My Stuff: My Continuum

←————————————————————————————————————→

    1   **2**   **3**   **4**

1. I wish I had more space in my classroom. There's just nowhere to store all my stuff. I can't throw things away. I might need them someday.

2. I don't have time to think about cleaning up my cabinets. I barely have time to do my lesson plans. But it would help if I could get my desk cleaned up. I'll use ideas from this chapter to help me with that.

3. I've been wanting to redo my storage area, especially my cabinets. During the break, I'll make that a priority and get started.

4. I realize that I must start with my storage spaces if I want to find room for all that's important in my classroom. I'm going to start with one storage space at a time and clean it out after school. There are probably lots of things I no longer need. If I just take one shelf a day, I'll be able to have this done in the next week or so.

Use with Chapter 1, Planning Your Space

PLANNING FOR MY SPACE

MY INSTRUCTION	SPACE I'LL NEED	THOUGHTS ON SETTING UP

Use with Chapter 1, Planning Your Space

MY FURNITURE INVENTORY

WHAT I'VE GOT	PURPOSE IT SERVES	KEEP IT	GET RID OF IT

Spaces & Places: Designing Classrooms for Literacy by Debbie Diller. www.debbiediller.com. Copyright © 2008. Stenhouse Publishers.

Use with Chapter 1, Planning Your Space

-------------------- **FURNITURE LIST** --------------------

Needed for Classroom of 25 Children (provided by school):

- 2–3 small tables
  - one for small-group instruction (with 6 kid-size chairs)
  - one for writing station
- 2–3 rugs to define spaces
  - large one for whole-group teaching area
  - smaller one for classroom library
- 25–27 student desks (or 5 tables) with student chairs
- 1 teacher desk (or small computer table to serve as teacher desk)
- 2 teacher chairs (with wheels preferably)
  - one for teacher desk area
  - one for small-group instruction area
- 1 two-sided Big Book/writing easel (one side used for teaching with big books and other side for modeling writing)
  - preferably dry erase/magnetic surface
  - large enough to accommodate Big Books and chart tablets
- 5–6 small bookshelves (could be built-in or freestanding)
  - two to three for classroom library
  - two for math manipulatives
  - one for other storage
- 1 overhead projector or document camera
- 4–6 computers for students to use
- cabinets for storage of teaching supplies
- cubbies for student storage of coats, backpacks, lunch boxes, etc.
- 3–4 pocket charts
- 1–2 tape recorders
- 2 file cabinets (shorter ones preferred)

Use with Chapter 1, Planning Your Space

THINGS I MIGHT BE ABLE TO LIVE WITHOUT

ITEM	WHY I DON'T NEED THIS	WHAT TO DO INSTEAD

Spaces & Places: Designing Classrooms for Literacy by Debbie Diller. www.debbiediller.com. Copyright © 2008. Stenhouse Publishers.

Use with Chapter 3, Come On In!

ESSENTIALS/ MUST-HAVES	OTHER THINGS YOU MIGHT LIKE HERE	LINK TO INSTRUCTION	MY PLAN
Whole-Group Area • large rug/carpet squares/mats to define whole-group teaching area • Big Book easel/writing easel • overhead projector or document camera on cart • calendar area for math	**Whole-Group Area** • comfy teacher chair (if you have space) • laundry basket for Big Book storage • small shelves for storing teacher materials needed for the day	**Whole-Group Area** • modeling how to read, write (and learn math, science, and social studies) • read-aloud, shared reading, modeled and shared writing, calendar work, group discussions, sharing time	**Whole-Group Area**

MY BEFORE PICTURE	MY AFTER PICTURE

Use with Chapter 3, Come On In!

ESSENTIALS/ MUST-HAVES	OTHER THINGS YOU MIGHT LIKE HERE	LINK TO INSTRUCTION	MY PLAN
Small-Group Area • table for small-group teaching • shelves or clear plastic drawer units for small-group reading materials behind the table • place this by a bulletin board/display space (to post anchor charts)	**Small-Group Area** • 6 dry erase boards and markers • tabletop dry erase/magnetic easel • 6 sets of magnetic letters (lowercase) • plastic tackle box for storing magnetic letters • anchor charts (developed with kids)	**Small-Group Area** • supporting 4–6 kids at a time as readers, writers, thinkers, mathematicians in small-group instruction • small groups for reading, writing, or math; literature discussion group meetings	**Small-Group Area**

MY BEFORE PICTURE

MY AFTER PICTURE

Spaces & Places: Designing Classrooms for Literacy by Debbie Diller. www.debbiediller.com. Copyright © 2008. Stenhouse Publishers.

Use with Chapter 3, Come On In!

ESSENTIALS/ MUST-HAVES	OTHER THINGS YOU MIGHT LIKE HERE	LINK TO INSTRUCTION	MY PLAN
Classroom Library • bookshelves • plastic shoeboxes or baskets for books • labels for book baskets (made WITH kids)	**Classroom Library** • small rug to define the space • silk plants • comfy kid-size chairs/pillows • lamp • display space for anchor charts on book choice and related reading strategies and book reviews	**Classroom Library** • place to self-select books for independent reading • cozy area to read in during literacy work stations • place to practice what we've been learning about: genre, authors, content, strategies	**Classroom Library**

MY BEFORE PICTURE

MY AFTER PICTURE

Use with Chapter 3, Come On In!

ESSENTIALS/ MUST-HAVES	OTHER THINGS YOU MIGHT LIKE HERE	LINK TO INSTRUCTION	MY PLAN
Writing Area/ Work Station • small table or two desks pushed together • trays for stacking and organizing paper • container for writing utensils	**Writing Area/ Work Station** • writing supports (dictionaries, thesaurus, writing models) • student mailboxes • fun kid-size chairs • bulletin board nearby	**Writing Area/ Work Station** • may be a place for materials to be stored for writer's workshop • space to practice writing during literacy work stations time	**Writing Area/ Work Station**

MY BEFORE PICTURE	MY AFTER PICTURE

Spaces & Places: Designing Classrooms for Literacy by Debbie Diller. www.debbiediller.com. Copyright © 2008. Stenhouse Publishers.

Use with Chapter 3, Come On In!

ESSENTIALS/ MUST-HAVES	OTHER THINGS YOU MIGHT LIKE HERE	LINK TO INSTRUCTION	MY PLAN
Other Literacy Stations • computers • ABC/word study • listening • Big Books • baskets or clear plastic containers for portable stations • "I Can" lists or directions written with students • management board	**Other Literacy Stations** • overhead, pocket chart, buddy reading, drama, poetry, etc. • materials to support above stations • tri-fold project boards (for portable stations) • storage unit for portable stations (wire cubes, milk crates, etc.)	**Other Literacy Stations** • places for students to practice reading and writing skills *previously taught* in whole group and/or small group	**Other Literacy Stations**

MY BEFORE PICTURE	MY AFTER PICTURE

Use with Chapter 3, Come On In!

ESSENTIALS/ MUST-HAVES	OTHER THINGS YOU MIGHT LIKE HERE	LINK TO INSTRUCTION	MY PLAN
Desks/Tables • student desks grouped together to save space (groups of 4–6) • teacher desk in small, out-of-the-way space (to maximize room for kids' learning)	**Desks/Tables** • might get rid of teacher desk and use small-group teaching table as desk, too (or use desk for double duty) • use small computer table as teacher desk	**Desks/Tables** • places for students to work independently to practice reading, writing, math, science, social studies, etc. • personal spaces for kids and for teacher	**Desks/Tables**

MY BEFORE PICTURE	MY AFTER PICTURE

Spaces & Places: Designing Classrooms for Literacy by Debbie Diller. www.debbiediller.com. Copyright © 2008. Stenhouse Publishers.

Use with Chapter 4, Using Your Walls

MY INSTRUCTION	WHAT I'LL DISPLAY	SPACES I'LL NEED/ CONSIDERATIONS

Use with Chapter 4, Using Your Walls

THINGS MY SCHOOL/DISTRICT REQUIRES ME TO DISPLAY	WHY IT'S VALUED	WHERE I'LL DISPLAY THIS

Spaces & Places: Designing Classrooms for Literacy by Debbie Diller. www.debbiediller.com. Copyright © 2008. Stenhouse Publishers.

Use with Chapter 4, Using Your Walls

OTHER THINGS I WILL DISPLAY	WHY IT'S VALUED	WHERE I'LL DISPLAY THIS

Reproducible Forms

Use with Chapter 4, Using Your Walls

THINGS I'LL EDIT/REVISE/NOT PUT ON DISPLAY THIS YEAR	WHY I'M DOING AWAY WITH THESE ITEMS

Spaces & Places: Designing Classrooms for Literacy by Debbie Diller. www.debbiediller.com. Copyright © 2008. Stenhouse Publishers.

Use with Chapter 4, Using Your Walls

ESSENTIALS/ MUST-HAVES	OTHER THINGS YOU MIGHT LIKE HERE	LINK TO INSTRUCTION	MY PLAN
Word Wall • cards with upper- and lowercase letters written on them (and picture cue for phonics in primary grades) • word wall words typed large enough (in black) for all students to see • low, interactive placement for students in pre-K, K, and grade 1 (so kids can see and reach words) • interesting words for vocabulary building in grades 2 and up • high-frequency words in pre-K through grade 1	**Word Wall** • shelves/stacking baskets for ABC/word study materials by the word wall • sorting space or large metal tray for sorts • place this near your ABC/word study station and your writing station, if possible, so kids can access these words	**Word Wall** • display for words we're paying attention to as readers and writers • make connections to these words while modeling how to read and write • use and spell these words correctly in your reading and writing throughout the day • in pre-K to grade 1, be able to take words on/off wall as you need them or want to explore them and how they relate to other words	**Word Wall**

MY BEFORE PICTURE	MY AFTER PICTURE

Spaces & Places: Designing Classrooms for Literacy by Debbie Diller. www.debbiediller.com. Copyright © 2008. Stenhouse Publishers.

Reproducible Forms

Use with Chapter 5, Organizing Your Stuff

MY LIST OF WHAT TO MOVE	MY LIST OF PACKING MATERIALS NEEDED

Spaces & Places: Designing Classrooms for Literacy by Debbie Diller. www.debbiediller.com. Copyright © 2008. Stenhouse Publishers.

MY SHOPPING LIST

Reproducible Forms

Resources

Staff Development Suggestions

Ten Plans for Professional Development

With the wide growth of Professional Learning Communities (PLCs), I often get requests for how to do follow-up training with the information I've shared. Here are ten possible plans for professional development that can be used in a wide variety of ways with *Spaces & Places*. You'll find specific suggestions for ongoing staff development, such as how to set up a yearlong book study. I've also charted ways to connect my literacy work stations videos *Launching Literacy Stations* (for K–2) and *Stepping Up with Literacy Stations* (for grades 3–6) to each chapter in this book. These suggestions can be used with the support of an administrator, a literacy coach, or a lead teacher.

Listed here are ideas for faculty meetings, embedded staff development time, and faculty room bulletin boards. Teachers love time to work on space and always ask how to get the materials I show for organizing. So I've included recommendations for how to provide structured release time and materials so often requested by teachers. Read through the suggestions, tweak them to match your staff, and choose what will work on your campus or school system. Let the learning begin!

1. Book Study

Use *Spaces & Places: Designing Classrooms for Literacy* in a book study. Have teachers meet by grade-level teams, an entire faculty, or as an ad hoc group of folks interested in this topic. Be sure each participant has a copy of the book. You might also give each of them a journal in which to jot down notes and ideas, a fun pen, and sticky notes to use while reading.

Ask teachers in the group to choose a chapter and then read and reflect on what they've read. (I recommend that you take it one chapter at a time.) Make copies of the charts in the back of the book that match the ones from the chapter they'll be reading and distribute these before they read. Then invite them to fill in these charts as they read and reflect on their classroom spaces. Plan a time for your next meeting and encourage teachers to bring back their notes, ideas, and filled-in charts.

Also, at the end of each chapter, you'll find a section called Next Steps/Things to Try. Challenge teachers to choose one or two of these items and try these. Ask them to bring back what they tried to your next meeting.

Or, you might have teachers read one chapter, bring back their notes and ideas, and then fill out one of the charts from the "Resources" section together. Another option is to meet after reading a chapter and take an item from the Next Steps/Things to Try and do it as a group in your meeting.

You might want to be strategic in how you read and study each chapter. Here's a possible calendar for the book study:

Chapter 1—"Planning Your Space" before school starts (June/July/August)
Chapter 2—"Arranging Your Room" during back-to-school time (August/September)
Chapter 3—"Come On In!" throughout the year
    Whole-Group Area and Classroom Library sections—September
    Small-Group Area section—October
    Literacy Work Stations section—November/December/January
    Desks/Tables—January
Chapter 4—"Using Your Walls"—February/March
Chapter 5—"Organizing Your Room"—April/May

Please note that any of the chapters could also be used at any time of year. *Any* day is a good day to get started with improving the use of space in a classroom!

However you choose to read and study the book, I do recommend that teachers work in a group or with a partner to get more from the experience. Book studies help our learning go deeper and can bring about lasting change. Enthusiasm is contagious.

2. Using Video Clips with the Book Study

As you study the book together, you might want to use clips from my video series, available from Stenhouse Publishers at www.stenhouse.com.

The next two pages list suggested clips and the series where you'll find them along with the chapter from *Spaces & Places* where you might want to use them.

3. Field Trips to Other Classrooms

As you read and study this book, it might be fun and informative to visit each other's classrooms. In other words, take a field trip . . . in your own school. As you read a chapter, have teachers take a field trip to another room to look for evidence of one element you've been exploring. For example, if you are looking at classroom entrances, have the group go together into classrooms, one at a time, and help each other problem-solve on each other's entryways. I've found we come up with the best ideas when we all put our heads together. I love when teachers borrow each other's wonderful ideas.

Another idea is to use the Scavenger Hunt Cards (found at the end of this section) in conjunction with your field trips. Give each teacher (or pair of teachers) a few of the cards and then ask them to visit other classrooms (at their grade level or anywhere in the school) to find examples of what's on the card. For example, they might look for "well-organized classroom library" or "innovative storage solution." They could take a digital camera along and snap photos to come back and share with others.

NOTE: An easy way to view digital photos is to put them in one file and then click on "View as a Slide Show." Use an LCD projector hooked to a laptop so everyone can see and discuss the photos together.

4. Structured Release Time

Whenever I do a workshop and talk about classroom space, teachers always say what they'd now like is *time* to work on their room arrangement or walls or storage areas. The problem is there's rarely time allo-

CHAPTER FROM *SPACES & PLACES*	SUGGESTED CLIP TO GO WITH IT (AND TIME)	DISCUSSION QUESTION(S)
Chapter 1—"Planning Your Space"	For more information on using the Instead Box, as pictured on p. 30, watch: • Instead Box Mini-Lesson (08:40)	How did the teacher involve students in solving the problem they had? Discuss student independence issues.
Chapter 2—"Arranging Your Room"	Observe room setup in the following clips: • First-Grade Progression, Work Station Time (03:25) • Second-Grade Progression, Work Station Time (03:50)	What do you notice about how the room is set up? How is every inch of space used?
Chapter 3—"Come On In!" and Chapter 5—"Organizing Your Stuff"	Look at each work station in the following clips (pause as needed, perhaps after every station shown): • First-Grade Work Stations Room Tour (05:30) • Second-Grade Work Stations Room Tour (05:30) For more info about the drama station, view: • First-Grade Progression, Mini-Lesson (08:05) For more info about the science/Big Book station, view: • Second-Grade Progression, Mini-Lesson (07:45)	What materials were used? How were they stored? How will this promote student independence? How did the teacher introduce the materials needed? What did you notice about organization/structure? How might these materials be stored?
Chapter 4—"Using Your Walls"	Look at the walls and the materials setup: • Literacy Station Progression (02:20) View the literacy management board in: • Two Stations in a Day Mini-Lesson (06:30) View how to make anchor charts with kids on these: • Second-Grade Friendly Letters Mini-Lesson (04:45) • Pumpkin Words Mini-Lesson (10:55) • Bubble Map Mini-Lesson (04:15)	What did you notice about the walls? What kinds of anchor charts did you see? What did the teacher do to make the management board easier to see/read/use? How did the teacher share ownership in creating the charts? How did she handle the variety of responses? How did whole-group teaching relate to practice at the literacy work station? How will the anchor chart help?

CHAPTER FROM *SPACES & PLACES*	SUGGESTED CLIP TO GO WITH IT (AND TIME)	DISCUSSION QUESTION(S)
Chapter 1—"Planning Your Space" and Chapter 2—"Arranging Your Room"	Look at the use of color and space in Lisa and Donna's rooms: • Third-Grade Work Station Time (08:17) • Fifth-Grade Work Station Time (04:22)	What did you notice about the colors in each room? How did the room feel? How are materials organized? What do you notice about how the room is set up? How is every inch of space used? How are portable stations used?
Chapter 3—"Come On In!" and Chapter 5—"Organizing Your Stuff"	Look at each work station in the following clips (pause as needed, perhaps after every station shown): • Third-Grade Room Tour (04:33) • Fifth-Grade Room Tours (03:33)	What materials were used? How were they stored? How will this promote student independence?
Chapter 4—"Using Your Walls"	Watch how each teacher uses the management board and how it is displayed: • Third-Grade Management Board (06:30) • Fifth-Grade Management Board (03:21) View how to make anchor charts with kids on these: • Fifth-Grade ABC Book Station (05:52) • Fifth-Grade Poetry Station (08:43)	What did you notice about the walls? What kinds of anchor charts did you see? What did the teacher do to make the management board easier to see/read/use? How did the teacher share ownership in creating the charts? How did she handle the variety of responses? How did whole-group teaching relate to practice at the literacy work station? How will the anchor chart help?

cated for this. Find creative ways to allow teachers to work on space solutions using *structured release time*. Give teachers time to create and then work with a specific plan or focus. Afterward, schedule a time to debrief and share what they've done.

For example, if you're reading Chapter 3, "Come On In!" ask teachers to choose one area they will work on, such as their small-group area or their classroom library or their teacher desk. Then have them create a plan, using this book and their discussions with colleagues. Next, give them a limited but reasonable amount of release time in order to start or complete their plan. (I've found that work expands to the amount of time we give it. Deadlines can be very helpful if they're realistic.) Check each teacher's plan before he or she goes off to work (to be sure it is doable in the allotted time). You might need to help to revise a plan if a teacher has taken on too much (or too little) at once.

Follow up the release time with a sharing time in order to debrief and provide accountability. Ask everyone to share what they did. You might even take a field trip to each room to see what was accomplished. Be sure to celebrate their successes, even baby steps. One clean shelf leads to another!

5. Classroom or Space Makeovers

I have facilitated many successful makeovers. The key is to start with a space that's manageable. I often ask administrators to choose one classroom per grade level. At times, we ask for volunteers. Other times, we've drawn someone's name out of a hat. Sometimes an administrator chooses whose room we'll work in. Nonetheless, here are some tips on how to successfully make over a space:

- Start small. If a teacher's room is really "full," just choose one area to redo. Get the teacher's input by asking, "What part of your room would you like to have a fresh start?" By beginning with what the teacher wants help with, you will be more apt to get buy-in that will sustain the effort afterward.
- If a teacher's room isn't too overcrowded (or in the summer when everything is removed), this is often a good place (and time) for a classroom makeover.
- I've found that many teachers need a storage makeover *before* a classroom makeover. Use the process in Chapters 1 and 2 of this book to redo the room. For a storage area makeover, such as the one near the end of Chapter 5, take just one space at a time. You might start with one storage cabinet or just a set of shelves. Take everything off to begin. (It will look worse before it looks better!)
- Always plan the space on paper first, involving the teacher whose room it is, and other teammates, if possible, for their input and for them to see the modeling. Then work together to move furniture. Often, the teacher adds final touches to the space after we've worked together (such as plants or special storage containers, labels, etc.).

6. Faculty Meetings

NOTE: Be sure to include all teachers in this investigation, such as teachers of art, music, P.E., special education, speech, and so on. Everyone can share ideas and benefit from this study.

You might want to spotlight teachers' study of space at a faculty meeting. To do so, here are a few ideas:

- Classroom Space Checklist—Together, work to create a checklist of what you might see when you walk through teachers' classrooms in the next few weeks based on the element of space you have been studying. For example, if you've been reading about and discussing wall space, chart together what they'll expect you to see in their rooms. Then type this up and use it to do a brief walk-through. Give teachers feedback after you've visited their classrooms and encourage them for their efforts. See a sample checklist in Figure R.1. A blank reproducible form is included at the end of this section.
- Door Prizes—These might be given to motivate teachers to continue to improve their teaching spaces. Give out the following kinds of door prizes at a faculty meeting (see the "Where to Find It" section for ideas):
  - Gift certificates from dollar stores, Wal-Mart, Target, or office supply stores (try to get these donated)
  - Cool storage containers
  - Organizational supplies (decorative file folders, magnetic bulldog clips, colored paper clips, clear plastic sleeves and a 3-ring binder, 3M Command hooks, etc.)
- Scavenger Hunt—Use the cards at the end of this section to send teachers on a hunt for organizational elements you've been studying together. You might give each group the stack of cards fastened together by a ring. Or give each group selected cards you'd like them to find.

  Give each group a digital camera and their cards and set them loose in the school to find examples of each card they have. First group back wins a prize (see Door Prizes for ideas). Or set a time limit and the group with the most examples wins a prize.

7. Faculty Rooms

Use the theme of "Spotlight on Space" to create a display in your faculty room. Post the current area you're studying, such as *small-group area* or *storage areas*, on a wall or bulletin board. Then invite teachers to post their photos, comments, questions, compliments, and so on, on this display. Be sure to contribute as well. Teachers will appreciate your involvement in this project. Watch the dialogue (and the learning) grow!

8. Materials Support

In "Where to Find It" you'll find many of the materials used in the classrooms pictured. Provide catalogs or allow teachers to go online to suggested sites to shop for materials needed. You might give each teacher or grade-level team a budget to work within. Tailor it to match what you've got. If you can only afford twenty-five dollars per room, it's a place to start. Most teachers are thankful for whatever they can get.

To help teachers get started, you might want to purchase the classroom mapping tool shown in this book from the Debbie Diller Design® line from Really Good Stuff at www.reallygoodstuff.com and use it in conjunction with Chapters 1 and 2 of this book.

Individually or as a team, you can write grants to get materials needed to organize classrooms. One of my favorite sources is www.donorschoose.org. Many local reading councils and even school systems have minigrants that can be written to get supplies such as those shown in the book. Or ask your parent-teacher organization for support. It's amazing what you can buy with funds from a cookie-dough sale!

You might even ask for donations from local stores or businesses to help your classroom space initiative. When I was teaching, I wanted to plant a garden with my class. So I took my school letterhead and teacher ID with me and went from store to store. Everything I needed got donated.

9. Lead by Example

Use your own office as a model. Take the ideas from this book and apply them to your work space. Let teachers know you are doing this and share your before and after photos with them! We are always modeling even when we don't think we're modeling.

10. Success Stories

I'd love to know what you've tried and how it's changed your teaching. Please send your success stories to me at www.debbiediller.com. And visit this site to read about what other teachers have tried, too.

------------------ FIGURE R.1 CLASSROOM SPACE CHECKLIST ------------------

WHAT YOU CAN EXPECT TO SEE	WHAT I'M TRYING	ADMINISTRATOR NOTES
• inviting, comfortable space		
• neat, organized area		
• labeled book baskets to help kids choose		
• variety of books, including fiction and nonfiction		
• rug to define the space		
• use of low bookshelves to help kids easily access books		
• anchor charts/resources posted in this area to help kids as readers		

Sample checklist brainstormed by teachers and administrators for Chapter 3, Focus: Classroom Library

WHAT YOU CAN EXPECT TO SEE	WHAT I'M TRYING	ADMINISTRATOR NOTES
• inviting, comfortable space	I like the way my library looks. I've added a lamp and rug. Also repositioned the shelves to open up my library.	I like it, too! I'd love to sit in your library and read a book.
• neat, organized area	This is still a challenge. I'm teaching my kids how to do this. Not there yet.	You'll get there. Let me know if I can help.
• labeled book baskets to help kids choose	This is my next step. I'll be adding these over the next 2 weeks.	You might take a look at Suzette's baskets. She may be able to help.
• variety of books, including fiction and nonfiction	Need more NF. I'll work on this with my book orders this year.	Check with the librarian. She has a few she can give you to get started.
• rug to define the space	Done.	Looks good.
• use of low bookshelves to help kids easily access books	Thanks for giving me these. Kids love them.	You're welcome!
• anchor charts/resources posted in this area to help kids as readers	We just charted how to choose just-right books.	Very explicit chart.

Sample checklist filled out by teacher and administrator/literacy coach for Chapter 3, Focus: Classroom Library

well-organized classroom library	inviting classroom library
neatly organized cabinets	room with 2 or fewer filing cabinets
thoughtful wall displays	hall display that informs parents

Spaces & Places: Designing Classrooms for Literacy by Debbie Diller. www.debbiediller.com. Copyright © 2008. Stenhouse Publishers.

Spaces & Places Scavenger Hunt Cards

innovative storage idea	anchor charts including elements on page 136
interactive word wall	storage that promotes student independence
teacher desk with minimal space	uncluttered corners (some white space)

Spaces & Places Scavenger Hunt Cards

organized small-group area	inviting whole-group area
neatly organized cabinets	unblocked classroom entry
double-duty furniture	use of just 2 or 3 colors in a classroom

Staff Development

---------------------------- **CLASSROOM SPACE CHECKLIST** ----------------------------

Chapter _____ Focus:

WHAT YOU CAN EXPECT TO SEE	WHAT I'M TRYING	ADMINISTRATOR NOTES

Staff Development